I0797049

# SITTING WITH DOGS

# SITTING WITH DOGS

STORIES OF RESCUE DOGS GOING FROM LOST TO **LOVED**

ROCKY KANAKA

**Publisher** Mike Sanders
**Art & Design Director** William Thomas
**Editorial Director** Ann Barton
**Senior Editor** Brook Farling
**Designer** Lindsay Dobbs
**Copy Editor** Claire Safran
**Cover Photographer** Navid Tavakolnia
**Proofreaders** Jean Bissell, Liv Peluso
**Indexer** Johnna VanHoose Dinse

First American Edition, 2025
Published in the United States by DK Publishing
1745 Broadway, 20th Floor, New York, NY 10019

The authorized representative in the EEA is Dorling Kindersley Verlag GmbH. Arnulfstr. 124, 80636 Munich, Germany

Copyright © 2025 Rocky Kanaka
DK, a Division of Penguin Random House LLC
25 26 27 28 29 10 9 8 7 6 5 4 3
003-350157-OCT 2025

All rights reserved.
Without limiting the rights under the copyright reserved above, no part of this publication may be reproduced, stored in or introduced into a retrieval system, or transmitted, in any form, or by any means (electronic, mechanical, photocopying, recording, or otherwise), without the prior written permission of the copyright owner.

No part of this publication may be used or reproduced in any manner for the purpose of training artificial intelligence technologies or systems. In accordance with Article 4③ of the DSM Directive 2019/790, DK expressly reserves this work from the text and data mining exception.

A catalog record for this book is available from the Library of Congress.
ISBN 978-0-5938-4958-3

DK books are available at special discounts when purchased in bulk for sales promotions, premiums, fund-raising, or educational use. For details, contact SpecialSales@dk.com

Printed and bound in Italy

**www.dk.com**

This book was made with Forest Stewardship Council™ certified paper – one small step in DK's commitment to a sustainable future.
Learn more at
**www.dk.com/uk/information/sustainability**

**TO THE SHELTER WORKERS**—THE TIRELESS WARRIORS

**TO THE SUPPORTERS**—THE BELIEVERS IN SECOND CHANCES

**TO THE VOLUNTEERS**—THE ONES WHO GIVE WITHOUT EXPECTATION

**TO THE ADOPTIVE FAMILIES**—THE HEARTS THAT OPEN WIDE

**FOR EVERY INCREDIBLE DOG** WHO HAS WAITED BEHIND A KENNEL DOOR, NOT KNOWING THAT LOVE WAS ON ITS WAY

**FOR EVERY WAGGING TAIL** THAT HAS FOUND ITS FOREVER HOME, AND FOR EVERY ONE STILL WAITING

***THIS BOOK IS FOR YOU***

**EVERY DOG DESERVES A CHANCE.** AND EVERY ACT OF LOVE, NO MATTER HOW SMALL, CHANGES LIVES.

# TABLE OF CONTENTS

# A VERY SPECIAL DOG SAVED MY LIFE—LITERALLY!

**I'm an early riser. One day in 2019, I got up like usual, took a shower, and got dressed. I was walking to the door to get my dog's leash for our morning walk when something hit me—hard, like I suddenly weighed a thousand pounds and my muscles had turned to wet noodles.**

I thought maybe I needed something to eat, but I was so lightheaded I needed to sit down, maybe even lie down. I shuffled toward the couch. The feeling was getting worse.

I was in my thirties and in good health. As horrible as I felt, it didn't occur to me that this might be serious. And then I saw Flip coming.

Flip was my seven-year-old Boxer and my best friend. He came bounding into the house from the backyard, with a look on his face I had never seen before. I could tell something was up. I just hadn't clued in yet that that something was me.

Flip jammed his nose into my knee, so hard I was worried he might hurt himself.

Whoa, what is wrong with this guy? I wondered. I thought maybe he was just excited to go for his walk, but he'd never done this before. His weird behavior was distracting me from the way I was feeling. He backed up and jammed his head into my knee again.

I was totally puzzled, trying to figure out what was going on in his mind, when it occurred to me: I was making him do this.

Flip wasn't trained to monitor anyone's health. But he was smart, and he and I did everything together. "Here come Rocky and Flip," our friends would say. We were inseparable, and he could tell as I stood in our living room, unsteady on my feet, that I was not myself.

I called to my wife, Kelly, who was down the hall in the kitchen: "Hey, something's really wrong. I need you to call 911."

I'm a jokester. Kelly was used to me goofing around. But making a joke about calling 911?!

"What are you talking about?" she called.

When Kelly stepped into the room and saw my face, she froze. Flip was still butting his nose into my leg. Kelly had lost her younger brother only months earlier, and, as I watched, the look on her face changed. She realized I was in real trouble. I knew what she was thinking: I'm about to lose my husband, too.

Whatever was happening to me, it was a shock to us both. Only two weeks earlier, I'd gone for my annual physical, and the results were so good I came home bragging that I was the golden picture of health! I was exercising regularly, often running ten miles on a whim, and generally taking great care of myself.

I asked her again to call 911. I wanted to tell Flip to stop butting into my knee before he hurt himself, but the words weren't coming out. I managed to sit down on the sofa. I felt like I was melting into the cushions. Somehow, my right hand still worked. I reached for the phone to dial 911. As much as I wanted to lay down, I was thinking that I had to stay upright. Whatever was happening to me, I had to stay present for Kelly's sake.

I looked at her. I said, "I love you." I was afraid those were going to be my last words, so I made sure to choose them carefully. I tried to say it again, to be sure she heard me, but all she heard was mumbling. I was having a stroke.

At first, Kelly felt panic set in. She's fit and strong, but I'm almost twice her size and getting me up off that couch herself wasn't going to be an option. She called 911. Busy signal. This wasn't looking good. She tried again and again until she finally got through.

I was very quickly in the back of an ambulance, rushing to the hospital. I spend most of my days caught up in the momentum of work–go, go, go. But strapped to the gurney, I was overwhelmed by the moment, grateful to be alive and thinking only that I wanted to be with Kelly and one day have a family. I guess I was thinking one other thing: If I made it out of this alive, Flip was getting so many treats!

That Boxer deserved all I could give him. He had alerted me to the stroke, leading me to call Kelly while I still had my voice. Had I sat down and tried to wait for the feeling to pass, she might have figured I'd left with Flip for our walk and not have found me until the stroke had done lasting damage. As it turned out, the doctors got to me in time. It would take a few months of rest and rehabilitation, as well as a procedure to close a hole in my heart to prevent future strokes, but I would recover completely.

Flip was my best friend. One hundred percent of the credit for me still being here, whole and healthy, goes to that sweet, goofy Boxer. If I hadn't known that face so well and had thought he was just being annoying and eager to go for his walk, I'd have been in deep trouble. That cheesy old saying about rescue dogs–we don't save them, they save us–was never more true.

Flip passed away four years after my stroke. There is nothing I will ever be able to do to repay him. And not just for saving my life that morning, but for everything he did to set me on the path I've taken in life. I'm trying to pay that debt, and I'll continue to try.

Sometimes, when people have a life-threatening health crisis, they emerge from it saying their life flashed before their eyes and they're now determined to do things differently. I emerged filled with gratitude that I had survived. A brush with mortality is a powerful reminder not to stress about the little or material things, and as I recovered, I found myself steadfast in the knowledge that I was on the right path, fostering dogs and working to build a family with Kelly. Inspired by what my loyal best friend had done for me, I knew that as soon as I was back on my feet, I was going to continue to give every ounce of my being to that path.

So every time I'm helping a shelter dog come out of their shell so they'll stand a chance of catching someone's attention and being adopted, I'd like to think Flip is proud of me. And when my time is through, I hope he and I will be together again, reminiscing about the morning when he saved my life.

If you're reading this book, there's a good chance it's because you've seen my show, Sitting with Dogs, or maybe some of the other creative ways I tell the stories of underdogs who need a family. And even if you haven't, thanks for picking up the book!

Dogs have been part of my life since I was a kid, growing up between Hawaii and the Midwest. While I was lying in the back of that ambulance,

I was determined to pay my dog back—I was determined to pay all dogs back. They make our lives better in so many ways. Yeah, Flip got some treats after that. But I wanted to do more, and that "more" is what this book is about.

Shelters are full of dogs that life just hasn't been kind to, and I've never seen shelters and rescues across North America as full as they are now in these years following the COVID pandemic. Inflation and the rapidly rising cost of living are making it harder to care for pets, and the cost of veterinary care is spiking along with everything else. The staff I've met in shelters are wonderful people. They give so much. But time is tight and the need is great. Shelter staff can't meet every need of every dog in their care. And a scared dog, trying to melt into the floor and disappear, can be its own worst enemy when strangers come through looking to adopt.

That's where I come in. Right in. Into the kennel with those frightened dogs. There's not a lot of room in those kennels for a guy who's six-foot-four, but I've learned ways to make myself as small and unthreatening as possible. If you've watched my show, you've seen how I do it. Little by little, calming those nervous pups and assuring them they're going to be okay. I might be able to spend only an hour with them—and it's not easy to leave at the end, believe me—but in that short time together, I'm often able to convince a dog that it's okay to open up and show their charming, loveable selves, so that next time a family walks past looking to adopt, that dog's not afraid to put their best paw forward.

It's now been more than a decade since I started helping dogs in shelters find their forever homes. Sometimes people ask how many dogs have been adopted as a result of this work, but the real answer is that there is no answer. It's the wrong question. Rescue is teamwork. It's a community. You'll meet dogs in this book who were adopted by people who saw the Sitting with Dogs videos, but the path from rescue to adoption went through the hard work and commitment of more people than just my team and me. They all deserve credit, and it would be impossible to count who among us has contributed to how many adoptions. I don't even try to keep track.

While getting dogs adopted is one goal, we hope *Sitting with Dogs* will inspire more people with big hearts and a little time to go down to their local animal shelter or rescue and offer to help. You might not be ready to squeeze right into a kennel with a nervous stray, but shelters are always looking for help of some kind. If I can inspire you to volunteer, foster, adopt, or use any skills you have to help, then I've done my job. If this book helps you understand how much good you can do by just getting started, even if it's in small doses, then it's done its job, too. Whether you are looking to change course in your life or have found some passion in helping animals, by getting involved you will find out what you're really capable of, and I promise it will be amazing.

Since first getting involved, Kelly and I have opened a dog rehabilitation center on our coffee farm in the countryside of Southern California. I'll introduce you to some dogs we've brought there to recover from their rough starts in life. I'll introduce you to many dogs I met only briefly, but who touched my heart in ways I'll never forget. And while you might be wondering if this will be a sad book or a hard book to read, I can assure you that this book is filled with happy adoption stories that will leave joy in your heart and hopefully inspire you to start, or continue, helping animals in your own way.

Although the experience of sitting in a tiny kennel with a dog might seem like it wouldn't change much from one day to the next, I've selected a variety of stories that make clear just how different each day can be. I'll tell you how I got started doing this, and I'll introduce you to dogs who taught me powerful lessons about friendship, helping each other face our fears, the value of living for the present, healing, the power of a name, bereavement, guilt and redemption, and resilience. And before I wrap up, I'll share some thoughts on why and how you can help in your own unique way, and I'll do so by sharing a little more about why and how I do what I do to help.

Some of those stories will make you laugh, some will make you cry. They'll all make you want to take these dogs home. That's what dogs do when we give them our attention and love. And I'm so, so lucky to have met so many. I hope you enjoy getting to know them as much as I did.

With Aloha,
Rocky Kanaka

# CHAPTER 1

# FLIP

# (THE DOG THAT SAVED MY LIFE)

SCAN TO LEARN MORE
ABOUT FLIP'S STORY

**Missy just showed up one day. My family and I posted signs around the neighborhood, trying to find who this beautiful German Shepherd belonged to. Nobody claimed her. As easy as that, at ten years old I'd found a new best friend.**

I was born in Hawaii, and my first dog's name was Kalei. (I don't remember her because I was so young.) When my family moved to Missouri we didn't have much money, so we kids often spent weeks at a time living and helping out on friends' farms so Mom could work. I got to know farm dogs, working dogs. Most were mutts, and they had enough smarts to make themselves useful. Some were treated like members of the family, while others were like employees who slept in the barn. I'd sneak them all leftovers from the table.

Missy was no farm dog. She became a member of our family, and in the way of things back then we built her a doghouse and she lived outside. I tried many times to bring her into the house, but that never went well. A dog that's never spent time indoors can find it scary inside. Missy would panic and run over the furniture, knocking things down. And why wouldn't she run around, excited? That's what she did everywhere else. She didn't know there were rules to being in the house.

Missy lived in the backyard but she didn't stay in it. She kept busting through the chain-link fence to chase rabbits and other dogs. German Shepherds are highly prey driven. They don't take well to idleness. So when we were at school, what else was she going to do but watch for things to hunt? We tried to bolster the fence, but she just jumped over it. I had watched farm dogs on the go, solving problems from sunup to sundown. Missy needed something to do.

We couldn't afford dog toys, but we figured out that if we buried our old toys in the sandbox, she would spend hours digging them out. Sticking her water bowl in the freezer overnight helped, too. She'd spend half the next day licking that big block of ice out of her bowl, chewing on it until it melted. We would often flavor it with ground beef, bone broth, or leftovers. That helped keep her out of trouble.

Trouble had followed Missy, though. Turns out she was pregnant. If my mother had ever considered getting her spayed, I'm sure she'd have found it unaffordable. There just weren't low-cost options back then. Fortunately, we had no trouble finding people to adopt her puppies. Few dog breeds are as capable of learning to work as German Shepherds. Farmers were happy to have them.

German Shepherds are smart, powerful animals. In a city, a dog as restless and clever as Missy might lead someone to take her back to the shelter, saying she's not listening or paying attention. Some dog owners don't understand why their shoes keep getting torn apart or why their dog keeps bolting out the door. Not many people appreciate what dogs are capable of doing. They get bored easily, and even little ones have an instinct for finding things to occupy their minds.

Over the decades, dogs have gone from being working animals to part of our families. Having a dog or any pet in your family is a learning experience and a journey. Missy taught me a lot about what we can do for the animals who live with us, and I try to pay that forward. Education for dog owners matters so much, and it's a big part of what I try to do when I advocate for adoption. Even pet experts don't just wake up knowing what they know. They learn over time and

***Me with my first dog, Kalei, in Kailua, HI.***

With my German Shepherd, Missy, and her puppies.

through trial and error, research, reading, and practice.

Unfortunately, not much of that education was happening back then. When Missy started to have hip problems, which were common for German Shepherds, and the vet told us we'd have to put her down, that's what we did. Today, a vet might help Missy live a few more years. But those were different times. And we could hardly have afforded the vet visits, let alone the thousands of dollars it would have cost to help her.

Missy wouldn't be the last dog I loved and lost. When I was about a decade older, my college roommate brought home a dog. Wendell quickly became my dog, really. When the school year was over and my roommate and I went our separate ways, I told him to call me if he ever wanted to get rid of Wendell, for any reason. I'd take him. A few months later, I saw my roommate and asked how Wendell was doing. I couldn't believe what he told me.

My old roommate had taken Wendell back to the shelter. He'd started circling obsessively then peeing on the floor, and my roommate figured something must have been wrong with him. The shelter was at capacity, and a dog with behavioral problems wasn't likely to get adopted. Wendell was euthanized.

There was likely nothing wrong with Wendell. Maybe with the circling he was showing early signs of dementia (unlikely, as he was young), or maybe he had an infection. But most likely he just needed someone to take care of him and show him the attention that every dog needs. Wendell wasn't getting that, so he acted out, hoping someone would notice. Someone did notice, unfortunately for Wendell.

That was a heartbreaker. But the lesson was sinking in. People need education about dogs. They need to know what to expect from a dog that's been in a shelter, and maybe never lived with a family before. And dogs need their new families to know that a lot of their antisocial behavior is just a manifestation of fear. Fear that we can counter with a bit of knowledge and love.

Another decade or so on, but still long before Kelly and I got married, she and I took a road trip about an hour north of Los Angeles to a little town in the mountains called Tehachapi. I was introduced to Zach Skow, who ran a dog rescue there called Marley's Mutts. Zach took in a lot of so-called bully breeds—big dogs who could be hard to get adopted from a regular shelter.

At the time, Marley's Mutts operated out of Zach's house, which is how rescues often operate, or at least how they get their start. I was excited to learn more about Zach's operation, so we loaded my Jeep with donated dog food to help him out.

As Zach was giving Kelly and me a tour, the most awkward little dog was following us around. He was sad and cute at the same time. This dog, a Boxer puppy, would take a few steps after me and then wipe out in a mess of long legs and big feet. Then he'd get up and do it all over again. He was only four months old, and everything about him reminded me of a cartoon character: big eyes, droopy ears, limbs out of proportion to the rest of his body, and skin that hung off him like he was a kid wearing his older brother's suit. And the way he was walking! Unsteady as a newborn calf.

Zach noticed me trying to make sense of this poor little Boxer. "Oh," he said, "that's Flip." I fell in love with him right then and there.

Like Flip himself, the name Flip was cute but also a bit sad. Zach filled me in. Flip got his name from the way he walked, because he had to

*Flip at the rescue the day I met him.*

Flip hanging out in the back of my Jeep, ready to go home the day I met him.

"flip" his paws over with each step. Before arriving just a few days ago, he had been kept in a crate that he had quickly outgrown, and the muscles in his feet and wrists were weak from inactivity and unnatural positioning. Imagine if you got down on all fours and turned your hands over so you were putting your weight on your wrists instead of the palms of your hands. That's basically how Flip's paws had been positioned as they developed. Pretty uncomfortable. Even though he was free now to walk around, his great big paws only straightened out if he flipped them into position with each step.

Flip wasn't deterred, though. He followed me around Zach's yard anyway, curious and stumbling every few steps but getting right back up. It's one of the things I love about dogs: They live in the moment. I could see that little Flip was going to learn how to get wherever he wanted to go, and if that meant wiping out while following this interesting new person around the yard, then he was up for it. No shame. No giving up.

As we finished our tour, I wasn't thinking of adopting Flip, cute as he was. It just wasn't on my mind. Flip had other ideas, I guess.

As we dropped the gate on the back of my Jeep to pull out the donations, Flip jumped in. Or tried to. The tailgate was too high, and those misaligned paws weren't getting him very far off the ground. He did a spectacular face-plant on the back bumper. True to his nature, Flip tried again. I helped him up this time, and he sat in the back of the Jeep like he was ready to go home.

Zach brought a blanket over and put it under Flip. The little dog was still dirty and didn't smell great. There hadn't been time yet to do a proper intake on him, including a bath. Flip didn't seem to notice. He sat looking at me with those big old Boxer eyes as if to ask, "Are you my dad?"

I guess I was. Boxers are high-energy dogs, but I was a runner so I wasn't worried about Flip getting his daily reps in. Zach cautioned me that those paws might never straighten out, and he reminded me that I was living on a boat in Marina del Rey, not most people's idea of the best place to raise a dog that would grow to 70 or 80 pounds.

Zach wasn't wrong to point that out. I was a young entrepreneur, trying to figure out where life was going to take me. I had a dream to work for myself and not need a nine-to-five job. I had recently expanded my store, The Dog Bakery, to multiple locations and launched it online. I'd also had some luck in real estate and bought and sold some other businesses. I was constantly on the move, working with no set hours, night and day. As much as I loved dogs, I wasn't in a great place to take one on. I didn't even have a yard.

I looked at Kelly and said exactly the thing that made no sense and for which I will be forever grateful: "I think I should take him. I want him. I think he's mine. He needs help."

But he had an appointment coming up with a veterinarian, so Zach held onto him until that happened. After the appointment, Zach would bring Flip down to me in LA. I couldn't wait to welcome him home.

~~~

The Flip who arrived ten days later wasn't the same dog I'd met in Tehachapi. The minute I scooped him up, I knew something was wrong. He had seen the vet, so I figured it couldn't be anything serious. But he wouldn't eat, and he had so little energy he could barely raise his head. I gently squeezed his paw, and when I let go the color wouldn't come back into the toe pads. Then he started coughing and wheezing. That determined little Boxer who'd followed me around Zach's house was nowhere to be seen.

Flip was already skinny, so I was worried. By nighttime, he couldn't open his eyes, and his breathing was worse. We rushed him to an emergency vet around midnight. The vet suspected Flip had distemper, a virus that spells the end for most dogs, as it attacks the respiratory, gastrointestinal, and nervous systems. The diagnosis was soon confirmed.

The vet let us know that this was probably it for my new little friend, and she and the clinic staff could take it from there. She told me the statistics, and the odds weren't in Flip's favor. The chances of him surviving were very small. But they weren't non-existent. "Let's try," I said. I figured we would know pretty soon if anything the vet did made a difference.

I threw down my credit card on the front counter and said, "Whatever it takes."

What it was going to take to even try was $1,200. But I didn't hesitate. The decision was made, whether it made sense or not.
~~~

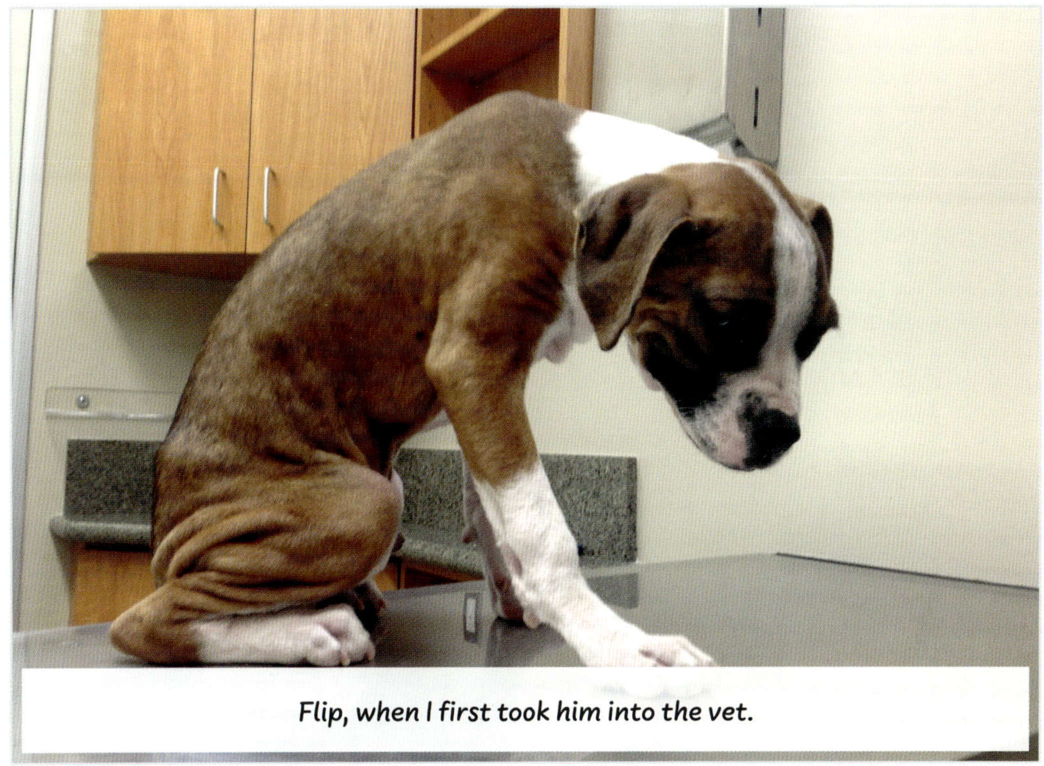

***Flip, when I first took him into the vet.***

The next day we checked in with the clinic. Flip hadn't improved. We came back the next day, and it was more of the same. I said, "Let's try again." Every time I said that, it cost me another $500. On the fourth day, the vet pulled me aside and said, "I know you're trying to do the right thing here, but this isn't working." For Flip's sake and mine, she thought we should accept defeat. I appreciated her candor, and I have no doubt that in most cases she'd have been right. But I wanted to give Flip one more shot.

When I'd met him only a few days earlier, it really felt like we were meant to be best pals for the long haul. I couldn't accept that he had gone through so much just to be euthanized because of a preventable virus. There's hope for every dog, at some point. Even against these odds.

I went home, hoping beyond hope but resigned to this being our last try. I returned the next morning, prepared for a tough day. I would stay with Flip and hold his paw until the end.

When Kelly and I walked in the front door, the staff were smiling. The vet said, "We've been waiting for you."

It took a few tries, but she managed to wake Flip from a very sound sleep. I put his little toy beside him. His head popped up and his eyes were bright. His little nub of a tail (his "finger tail," I called it) was wheeling around. This was the first time I experienced the feeling of a dog beating the odds stacked so high against them, and little did I know that Flip would return this favor one hundredfold.

"We're not out of the woods yet," cautioned the vet. But Flip was starting to eat again and had clearly turned a corner. Within 24 hours, he was running around the clinic and making friends with the staff. The bill might have ended up around $10,000, but it was the best money I've ever spent.

Flip still had health issues. He needed to put on weight, and we had no idea whether we'd be able to correct his paws. But as we took him home from the clinic, none of that mattered. We got him on the boat, and he was as happy and bouncy as a Boxer puppy should be. Kelly had a couple of dogs too, and he was excited to meet them. Any concerns about living on the boat went away when he curled up in a little donut-shaped dog bed and fell fast asleep.I'm home, he seemed to say. I've got this.

Over the months ahead, we worked really hard to help his paws, muscles, and joints heal through regular exercise, diet, and rehabilitation. He was still growing, which I'm sure helped. Boxers aren't great endurance athletes because their short noses make breathing less efficient and don't help regulate body temperature like a longer snout does. I was a runner, and this was Los Angeles. It was usually hot. This was Flip, though, and thanks to all our rehab work, he got to the point where he could run five or six miles with me. That was impressive! In the hot months, we would run in the early mornings or nights so that he wouldn't overheat. I'd take him to my boxing class, and he'd get upset whenever the instructor took a swing at me. We did everything together. He'd sit with me on a restaurant patio and greet everyone as they came and went. The neighbors got to know and love him like he was their own.

Flip was just *that guy.*

With Flip recovering at home and The Dog Bakery business expanding, I wanted to find more ways to help dogs. So I started doing adoption days at the bakeries, and any time

*Flip went to the bakery with me every day.*

Me and my best friend in Marina Del Rey, CA.

we got a dog adopted, my team and I were overjoyed. We loved the dog birthdays and Barksgivings, but seeing a shelter dog go home with a new forever family? That was next level.

The tough part came with the relentlessness of it all. For every dog we got adopted, many more were showing up at the shelters. I started going around to shelters in LA and asking what more we could do to help. Of course, no one had an easy answer, but if we could convince more people to adopt instead of automatically going to a breeder, that would get lots of dogs out of shelters and into homes where they would be loved.

As time went on, Kelly and I started taking dogs into our home, fostering them, and helping spread the word that they needed adoption. We discussed sharing some of these fosters on social media, because we were sure other people out there might want to help, too. At the time I don't think we had any idea how true this would turn out to be. We started small: We took a shelter dog to the beach, where he howled like Chewbacca from Star Wars when he saw the ocean for the first time after being locked on a chain for the first five years of his life (Teddy "Bear" Herschel for any of my longtime followers out there). We took an unbelievable little double-amputee dog for a hike in the woods. We wanted to show people these dogs and make them think of how much better life could be sharing it with one of them.

Shelters were glad for the extra attention, especially for the dogs who were hardest to adopt. Sharing videos of the dogs' stories was helping them get adopted, but we knew we needed to do more because there were so many dogs depending on us.

Taking dogs out on amazing days (my show called *Dog's Day Out*) to highlight some of the great animals available for adoption and sharing our overall foster journey was amazing, but one thing kept sitting heavily on my heart. Many people have the idea that shelters are dark, dreary, sad places. When I'm in a shelter, I am most often surrounded by amazing staff, volunteers, happy animals, amazing moments of pets being reunited with their families, unbelievably joyful adoptions, and more. Yes, sometimes battles are lost or a story is hard to hear or see, but on most days the wins outweigh the hardships.

I kept sharing videos of what life was like in the shelter, but they weren't connecting the way I was hoping. It was a very strange thing, because a lot of people were watching–hundreds of thousands to millions–but we weren't seeing a big increase in adoptions. Sometimes it worked, but I knew I wasn't doing a good enough job of showing what the shelters are really like. I reached a point where I wanted to give up. I remember the specific moment I was feeling defeated by all of this, because it was when I met a German Shepherd named Princess.

I said to Kelly, "I'm not sure if she's going to let me work with her. I'll just sit with her for a bit. No need to record." We had a Canon camera but we didn't turn it on. I did, however, always set up my phone in the kennel, as I use it as a rearview mirror of sorts so I don't have to make eye contact with the dog. I also thought I would hit record on the phone so I could maybe show some of our really engaged members what sitting with a dog is like behind the scenes when I'm just assessing the dog's state of mind and taking some time to give them the love they deserve regardless of the pending outcome.

"This video's a little bit different," I said at the beginning. "But if you like it, I'll take you along on more of these." I was staying positive. For us, it's really about the dog's story and community versus the views and content. I hoped this amazing dog would feel the love I was trying to give her during the time we spent together. And that was most important.

Like I mentioned, I set my phone on the floor in front of me to function as a rearview mirror. Princess would have been too intimidated had I faced her when I entered the kennel, and that could

**_Princess, the German Shepherd._**

have led to her lashing out or withdrawing further. The phone lets me watch how she's reacting to my presence while I take the pressure off her by facing the door.

Princess looked healthy and well groomed. Her nails were trimmed, and she didn't have the grey creeping into her facial fur that dogs usually get by the time they're eight, which was Princess's age according to her intake card. She was nervous though, curled up in a back corner, shaking. I'd have to take it easy with her. Being closed in a tiny kennel with a nervous German Shepherd could go really wrong, and quickly.

With that in mind, I squatted at the front of the kennel. If she became aggressive, I could stand quickly from this position and use my handy dog lead I wear around my shoulder. Sitting immediately would be too risky, until I knew she was going to remain calm.

I'm partial to the power of dog treats, and not just because I bake them myself. They really can serve as a great entry point for helping a dog become comfortable with you. I was heartened when Princess took a treat from me almost immediately. She nearly took my fingers with it though. You can tell if a dog has been given food from a person's hand before, because they won't chomp your fingers along with the treat. Princess was a chomper. No harm done. She was just untrained. And I will say from experience, German Shepherds are some of the worst hand feeders. They get overexcited for that delicious treat!

Feeling comfortable with her after a few minutes, I sat down. Her ears were up, which was a good sign. She was alert without indicating fear. She clearly wanted to be friendly. Then she let out a big whoof of a breath. She was releasing tension. I tried to look at her, but she immediately turned away. It was too soon for eye contact. But she did start sniffing around for more treats. Although other dogs barking and crying kept getting her guard up and setting us back a little, we were making progress.

I had to catch myself a couple minutes in. I was sitting with this beautiful German Shepherd who seemed friendly, despite her fear, and who showed every sign of having been well loved. Because she was microchipped, the family had been notified she was in the shelter. So why was she here? Dwelling on the possible answers to that question can really sink you, and thinking about what had landed Princess in the shelter got me

**_Princess, scared, just wants to melt away._**

feeling low. But it's moments like that when the dogs work their magic.

Princess let me look at her, and that was great because I saw how she reacted when I said her name out loud. Her eyes lit up! I took the opportunity of handing her treats to pet her. We were really burning through my jerky sticks. Soon she was taking the initiative to check me out, sniffing, looking for more treats. Her anxiety was waning, but I had to keep my cool. She would pick up on my energy, and there wasn't enough space for us both in there if she got excited.

When I left the kennel, I hoped she would follow me to the door. That would make it harder to leave, but it's a good sign because it means the next time people come through the dog is more likely to step forward and act friendly.

Princess retreated to the back of the kennel. Even a treat through the bars couldn't entice her. I made a mental note to see her again.

On my way back home, I decided I was only going to release this to the small community that has been a part of this from the start and add captions to the video to help members understand what I was saying. Because the shelter noise was so loud, I questioned even doing this. But members on our channel pay a small monthly fee for special content and to be a part of us helping more dogs, so I thought this might be valuable to them. Then I had an idea. What if I could run this through an audio AI filter to reduce the background noise?

Suddenly, you could hear me and Princess, and a little bit of Kelly and our producer, Alexis, who were just outside the kennel door. I wondered, what if I just shared this? I showed Kelly, who is the most supportive wife imaginable, and she said, "I know you're great, but are you 30 minutes of great?" She had a point. The video was all me and Princess, nothing else. I posted it anyway.

Exhausted, I took a nap with our baby daughter, Capri. By the time I woke up, the video was exploding! People were asking in the comments for more like it.

"I think we're getting this dog adopted," I said. Kelly watched the video and realized that showing the process of how we learn about the dogs was intriguing, and simply slowing down and sitting with Princess allowed her to shine.

There were certainly comments from people wondering why I didn't have all the answers about Princess's story or why I didn't just make a video of the dog, but the

**Princess starts to look to me for guidance.**

majority of the people appreciated how such raw footage gave Princess the opportunity to be seen and hopefully adopted. And guess what? It worked. Princess was adopted, and she led the way for many more adoptions to come.

The lesson I learned with Princess is that dogs are so forgiving and will give us leeway to try new things. Most dogs are there for you no matter how many times you mess up, so don't be afraid to just try. In most situations with your dog or a dog you're helping, they only need you as you are in that moment, not the person you want to be one day. It's why they are so amazing. Like a best friend, they accept you for who you are right now and believe you are whole and perfect. So often I find myself focusing on what I need to do to improve, but my dog knows I am fine just the way I am.

***Princess starting to trust me enough to take treats.***

*Flip ready to play fetch with me.*

# CHAPTER 2

# CASPER

## (FIGHT, FLIGHT, AND FREEZE)

SCAN TO LEARN MORE
ABOUT CASPER'S STORY

**Shelters can overwhelm you. Just the emotion of those places. All those dogs who have been lost, surrendered, or just abandoned. There's so much sadness in those kennels, I have to be careful not to let it get the better of me. Of course, there are also moments of joy, when the shelter system works and a dog goes home, with their old family or a new one.**

But when I walk through the kennel rows, no emotion feels as heavy in the air as fear. The dogs don't know where they are or why they're there. Or worse, the dogs have been there before, and now they're back and feeling the sting of their rejection by the family that had once adopted them. Even with shelter workers doing their best to check in on all the animals, it's lonely being locked in a kennel, surrounded by other scared and noisy dogs.

One dog wouldn't be alone in his fear, however. In the case of a Dogo Argentino called Casper, who was absolutely petrified, I had to deal with fear of my own until a staff member walked through the kennel door and saved the day—and maybe saved Casper, too.

---

I see a lot of struggling dogs. So it was no surprise when I walked into the shelter one day and was told immediately by staff that they had a new arrival named Casper who could really use my help. I made my way down the kennel row, thinking I'd be able to identify the dog when I saw him. I was right. I passed a few others who seemed to be managing well enough. Then I saw a very large Dogo Argentino and knew immediately that this was the animal the staff were talking about.

It was eerie, the way he was standing stock still in his kennel, almost as if someone had told him not to move. Freezing in place like that is a sign that the dog is terrified. But Casper wasn't just frozen in fear. He was standing in front of the kennel door, as if waiting for his family to return. His posture made him look totally heartbroken and would make anyone want to enter that kennel and comfort him. But through the eyes of someone who spends a lot of time around dogs who are under stress, his posture was also deeply concerning.

A Dogo Argentino isn't the largest of dogs, but they're big enough, often around 100 pounds. They are powerful animals, bred in South America to hunt boar and puma. And they're strikingly beautiful.

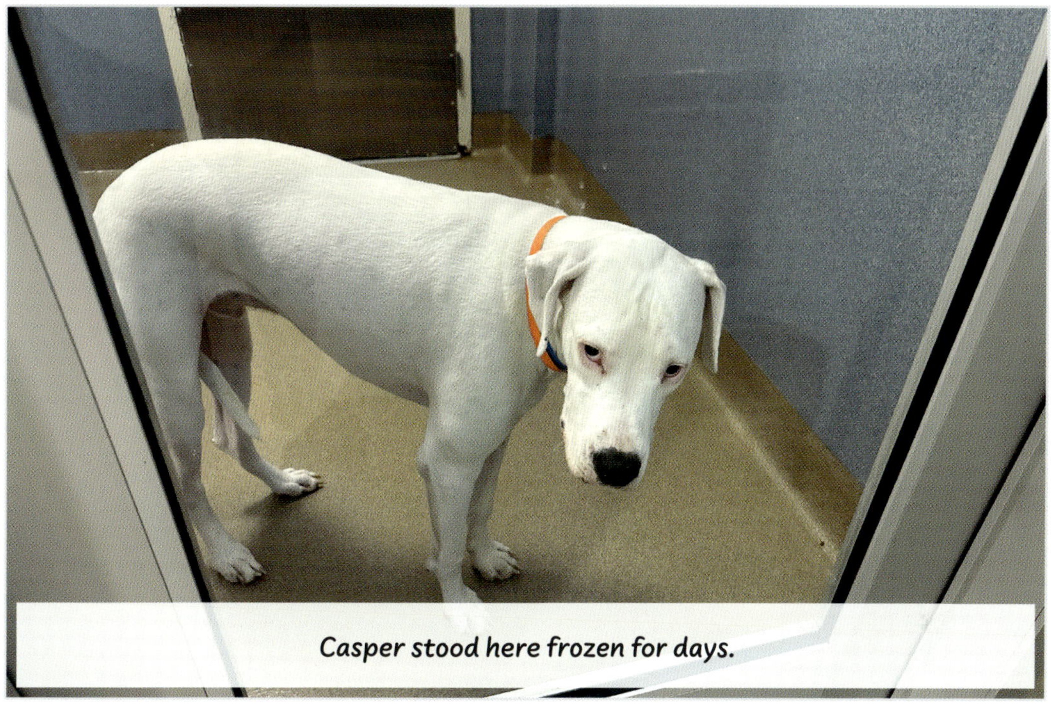

**Casper stood here frozen for days.**

Casper was all white, except for a hint of black on the tips of his floppy ears. We'll never know what, if anything, he was mixed with, but he was unusually long and lean and not quite as square-jawed as the breed is typically. His long tail was tucked tightly between his legs, another sign of fear. But most revealing was the drool.

You expect a big Saint Bernard or a Mastiff to slobber all over you. Many big dogs do. Dogo Argentinos do a bit, but nothing like Casper was. Long strings of drool hung from his jaws, and he wasn't shaking them off, which was a further sign that stress had taken over. I was sad to see him like that, but also hesitant.

When I see a big dog–especially one bred for power–in a state of fear, it sets off alarm bells. That's not how they are supposed to be. You expect to see their head held high, poised to protect their family and be a reliable companion and best friend. Dogo Argentinos are excellent pets (though ideally when kids are a little older). So the prospect of entering the kennel with a dog behaving so strangely in that fear state was messing with my mind. I was going to help him, but I had to manage my own emotions while trying to figure

ANIMAL FRIENDS OF THE VALLEYS
33751 MISSION TRAIL
WILDOMAR, CA 92595
Phone: (951) 674-0618

Shelter pets ... heads and tails above the rest!

Kennel Card

Animal Profile for CASPER

| | |
|---|---|
| Species | Dog Id#: 668036 |
| Breed | Dogo Argentino |
| Age | Adult Dob: 08-09-2022 1 Yrs, 4 Mos |
| Gender | Male/sterilized |
| Color | White |
| Size | Xs - 2-25 Lbs |

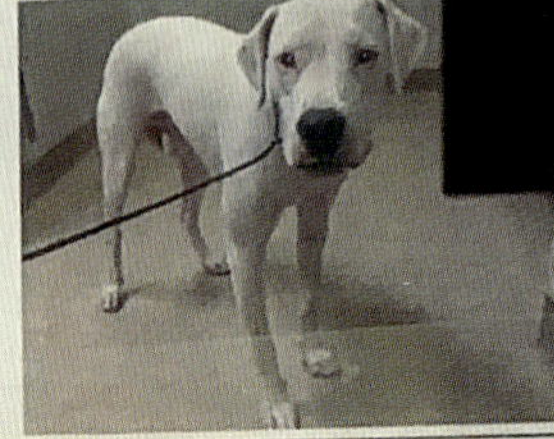

Case 12-09-2023.1 Status: Owner Known DA12

| | | | |
|---|---|---|---|
| Arrival Date | 12-09-2023 | Condition | Fair - Not Sterilized |
| Arrival Reason | Owner Turn In | Re-evaluate | - - |
| Transport | Abandoned-night Drop | Collar | Nylon Green |
| Aco | | | |

Hello!

I am new here.

I am very scared and still getting used to my new surroundings. Please no visits at this time.

Animal care staff is working

*Casper's warning note on his kennel card.*

out how to get through to him. The hardest part, though, was getting a read on his state of mind. Was he ready to tear into me or would I frighten him even worse when I entered the kennel? Standing in place like that, he was giving me no indication of how he might react.

---

If you dismiss the fear you experience when you encounter a big dog, or even a smaller one whose response to you is unpredictable, I think you're fooling yourself. I've never really been scared of dogs, at least under ordinary circumstances, but it's worth talking about those moments when it's perfectly reasonable to be at least a little scared. The times I've felt fear because of a dog have mostly been under stressful and unusual circumstances. I've worked with hoarding-case dogs, dogs that are shut down, and others that are lashing out. I learned over time how to anticipate trouble from a mix of environmental and behavioral signs. But Casper was giving me nothing. Zero. I had no idea what I was in for. With a dog his size, let's be honest, that was a scary moment.

Casper was so firmly planted in front of the kennel door, I entered the kennel through its back door. It was a big kennel, fortunately, with lots of space for us both. He turned to face me but otherwise resumed his frozen posture. He tracked my movement with slow turns of his head, but that was all the motion I was getting out of him. I didn't greet him. I kept my hands tucked in my pockets trying to look casual. I inched my way around to the front of the kennel with my back to him, avoiding eye contact. He wasn't going to make eye contact in return, but trying to force that connection too soon might set him off.

This was not my usual upbeat approach! Still, I wanted to stick with my usual techniques when I sit with a new dog, because through trial and error I've learned the fundamentals work best. Part of it is talking out loud, if not to Casper then to myself or anyone who will listen. That lets a dog know I am there just to hang out, no pressure.

When I started sitting with dogs, I noticed that silence leaves an uneasiness hanging in the air. Entering the dog's space in silence was no better than bursting in making baby talk and overwhelming the dog. You wouldn't react well to a stranger suddenly approaching you like you were their best friend, and a silent approach–especially if the stranger was staring at you–would make you at least suspicious and very likely defensive. So, whether I'm talking or humming a song, I try to create a situation where the dog doesn't feel like the center of attention. I've sat and read aloud to a nervous dog, just to show through my tone of voice that I was on an even emotional keel.

Really, what I needed to do for Casper was the opposite of what he was doing for me: give him lots of behavior to evaluate, so he would eventually feel comfortable letting down his guard and opening up to me.

He stayed frozen in place, and so did I. Though he wasn't giving any signs of aggression, I had to remind myself that a frightened dog's behavior can be as unpredictable to the dog itself as it is to me. He needed time for whatever was going on in his mind to work itself out. Even though he kept an eye on me, he'd only glance, then turn his head away, hoping if he ignored me maybe I'd disappear. I noticed how downcast and glossy his eyes were. I suspected he hadn't slept in days.

I get asked sometimes whether I've ever been bitten by a dog. The answer is yes. You learn a few things

***Casper creating as much space as possible.***

***Me trying to give Casper some affection.***

from a dog biting you. One, you learn how to get bit. If a dog grabs onto your forearm, which has happened to me a few times, you don't pull away. You push your arm into it, so the teeth don't tear your skin when you pull away. There are a few little tricks like that. But the biggest thing you learn is how to keep a dog from biting in the first place.

Bites are almost always avoidable. I say that, and I'm working in some extreme places with dogs who are very anxious and uncomfortable. Sometimes when I step into a kennel, the dog's instinct to bite is just one little misstep away. But I almost always manage to avoid it. And you should too, because a dog's life can depend on it.

In most shelters across the U.S., if a dog bites, it may be a death sentence for the dog. Shelters are often at or beyond capacity; they don't have the resources to figure out why a dog is biting and how to stop it. Besides that, a dog that bites can be a legal liability. In some jurisdictions, a dog could even be in its home, and if it bites, it's game over.

So it's not just a fear of pain that was making me afraid of Casper biting me. I didn't want anything more to happen to Casper. Who knows what had made him like this. My job was to help him turn a corner in his life and send him on his way to his forever home, not a dead end.

I tried everything.

Once I was confident Casper wasn't going to lash out, I crouched down low against the far wall. I wanted him to lead, at his own pace and when he was comfortable. He continued to show a flicker of curiosity, but otherwise—nothing.

I reached slowly around to my back pocket for a jerky stick. He caught wind of it and gave a few sniffs, but when I crumbled some pieces on the floor in front of him, he didn't budge. I offered a piece by hand. He sniffed again but turned away. I tried offering some bits in my palm, but he didn't even look. Positive affirmations went right past him. I finally sat. He watched me change position but didn't move an inch himself. I turned my back as if I were totally uninterested in him, which made me a little more nervous, but his feet remained firmly planted. I even tried singing. Not that I'm a great singer, but my daughter had

Casper getting a little closer.

recently come home singing "This Little Light of Mine," so the words and tune were fresh on my mind. I tried. I'm sure all the other dogs enjoyed it. But Casper? Nothing.

~~~

At this point, I was more afraid of Casper's story than the dog himself. What horrible experience could make him act this way?

When I meet a new dog, I like to go in with very little information, so other people's impressions won't influence my read of the dog's behavior. A shelter worker can spend just a few minutes with a dog before they go into a kennel, and if in those moments the dog is scared and acts out, those few seconds of bad behavior might be the only thing I hear about the animal. So I ask for just the essentials: whether he has shown signs of aggression or is injured and can't be touched in certain places.

But since getting in that kennel with Casper, I'd emptied my toolbox. It was time to hear this dog's story. Fortunately, Alexis had been talking to the staff who had received him and taken him through his health check. Casper, she learned, had been left in night drop.

Night drop is a stacked row of small, stainless-steel cages, accessible to the public after hours. It's meant for stray dogs and cats and injured wildlife found by people who can't hold onto them until the shelter opens in the morning. The rules for leaving a dog in night drop are posted in giant red and black text right on the door. Being left there is scary for the animals, but better than being left on the streets.

What night drop is not meant for is owners who want to dump their pets. That's abandonment.

Casper had appeared in night drop with no note, nothing to identify him or explain why he was there. Surveillance video wasn't helpful, but fortunately, he was microchipped. That's how I learned the saddest part of Casper's story: He'd been adopted from this same shelter about a year earlier, almost to the day. In fact, the shelter staff had named him Casper the first time he'd been left in night drop.

The shelter tried to contact his family. The only response was an email saying his family didn't want him and not to contact them further.

And here was Casper, standing vigil, waiting for them to return. The sadness in the kennel was just
~~~

crushing. I could feel the loyalty in him, the faith he had in his family, that they would come back and take him home, just as they had a year ago. Worse, if he had a health or behavioral problem the shelter needed to know about, they'd never find out now.

Now that I knew Casper's story and why he was so distraught, I could start to work through it. The problem remained, however, that I didn't know where to begin.

You see a lot of fight and flight in dogs; when they're scared, sometimes they bare their teeth or sometimes they just run for it. But there's nowhere to run in a shelter, and the fear and cramped quarters can take the fight out of even a big dog like Casper. That's when I started to notice a third fear response during my time with shelter dogs, one that nobody talks about: freeze. I was seeing it now, and I was really starting to doubt that Casper would ever thaw out.

I thought about trying to take him for a walk, but that much pressure could leave him no choice but to bite. And he was already standing, so it's not as if he was hiding in a corner, as I see lots of scared

*Casper begins to inspect me.*

668036

dogs do. As I was trying to think of other options, Casper's head was drooping lower. He could barely keep his eyes open. It was clear to me by this point that he really had been awake since being dropped here two days earlier.

I tried switching up the energy with some more positive affirmations, which got him to turn his head my way, but nothing more. I was ready to leave him alone for a while, in case my presence was just too much for him to process.

Almost like a movie, where good things finally happen at the characters' lowest moments, Casper's head lifted. He'd picked out a sound from the constant noise around his kennel. A voice. It wasn't mine. But for the first time since I'd joined him in that kennel, a light came into his eyes.

Through the glass door, I could see Kelly talking to someone in the hallway, but I couldn't see who. I signaled to her to encourage the person to come to the door, because Casper was finally–*finally!*–showing signs of breaking his freeze.

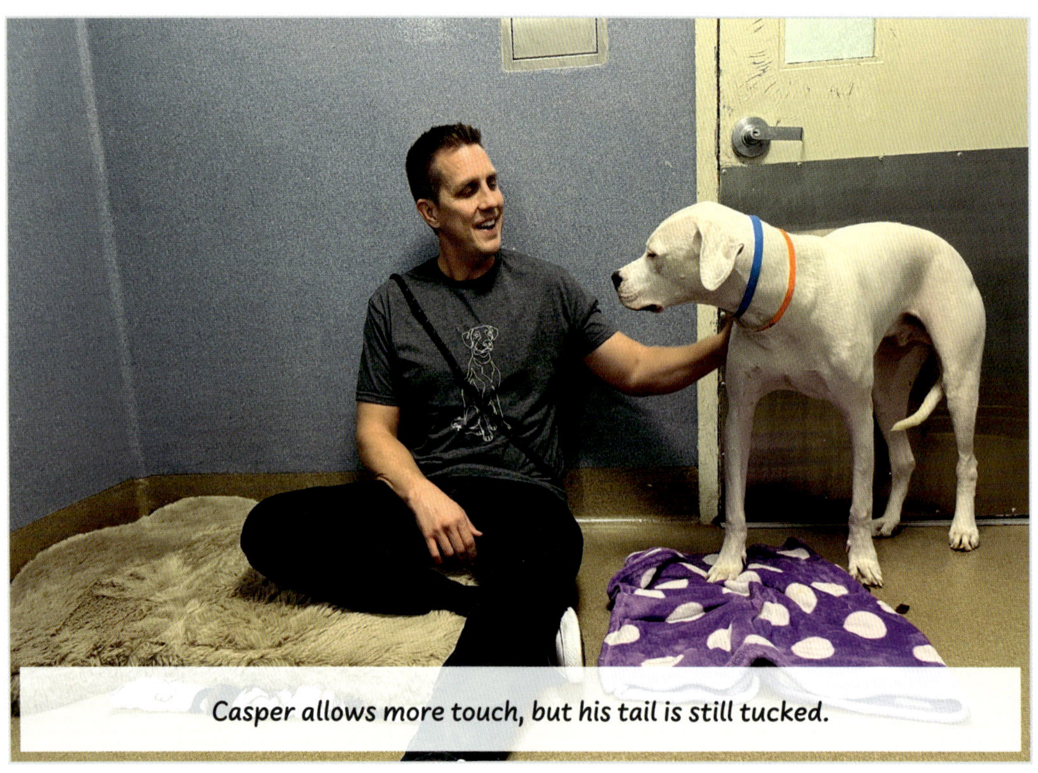

**Casper allows more touch, but his tail is still tucked.**

In walked Jennifer, staff animal care specialist, and within a minute Casper went from frozen on his feet to collapsing against her as she sat on his blanket. His tail was still tucked between his legs, but he was sniffing and licking her face, behaving suddenly like an ordinary dog. It turned out Jennifer was working the day he'd arrived, and I believe she even knew him from the first time he was at the shelter. She had somehow cut through the anxiety that was petrifying him, and now she was back. And Casper was a dog again!

Amidst all the nuzzles and licks, a question occurred to me: What would happen when Jennifer left? Casper wasn't showing any signs of being afraid of me, but when I offered him my hand for a sniff, he turned immediately back to Jennifer.

It's human nature to feel a little scorned after you put yourself out there only to be rebuffed for someone else. Some people want to be the hero; they want to be the person who wins an abandoned dog's trust. But this effort can't be about me. It's not about who the dog trusts, it's about helping the dog trust again. It's about getting them out of this state of being shut down and unshakably sad. There are Jennifers in every shelter working little miracles like she'd managed with Casper, and we should all be grateful for them.

Not that she minded making the effort! "They didn't ask to be here," she said, meaning the dogs. "I'm always happy to give them my love. It's free!" Most people aren't comfortable being on camera. But this moment with Jennifer not only helped tell Casper's story, it was a glimpse of the amazing attitude that shelter staff bring with them every day.

As Jennifer filled me in on Casper and he was smothering her in kisses, I was thinking of potential adopters walking past and seeing this big teddy bear rather than the terrified dog I was confronted with half an hour ago. With that difference in mind, we took a picture of Jennifer and Casper together to post on the kennel window. If later he went back into his fear state, at least adopters could see how loving he could be.

Jennifer couldn't stay forever, as much as Casper wanted her to. This was the real test of his turnaround. It was back to just him and me. He was sitting now, at least, not standing by the door. I reached over to offer my hand, and he backed away a little but let me pet him between the shoulders. He didn't seem scared now so much as cautious. Fair enough. But this was progress, and as moments passed he let me pet his chin and came closer to where I was sitting. Pretty soon I was getting kisses, too.

I don't normally let a new dog lick my face. Not because it's gross (though an affectionate dog can get *real* sloppy real quick!). But because human faces are hard for a dog to read. Subtle changes (and your face *will* change when it's getting licked) can communicate to a dog in ways we don't intend or understand, changing their attitude and even leading to aggression. And if the dog's snout is blocking my view, I can't read changes in the dog's body language. If there's trouble brewing, I wouldn't see it coming.

Kisses from Casper were worth the risk. I was just so happy to see the change in him, and I wasn't going to shut it down right away. But I did move him on to rubs and pets before too much time had passed. It was better to be safe, for his sake.

He stepped into my lap and just melted. It was one of my happiest moments in a shelter, ever.

***Casper happy with his new family: Murray, Luca, and Riley.***

A moment later, his head hanging over my arm, he closed his eyes and fell asleep.

---

"We have good news and bad news."

This is not how I want a call from the shelter to begin.

Although there weren't a lot of people who could take a giant fearful dog with serious anxiety, a couple named John and Michelle had filled out an application to adopt him. That was good news. In fact, it was more than good news–it was great news! What could be wrong?

He had kennel cough.

Kennel cough is a respiratory disease that can spread like wildfire through a crowded dog shelter. You might also have heard it called Bordetella. Most dogs pull through in a week or so. But to an animal with a weak immune system, it can do real damage, up to and including not surviving.

Casper looked healthy and was only a year and a half old, so his prospects of surviving should have been good. But the stress he'd been under could have run down his immune system. And the deep sadness he'd been feeling made me wonder whether he would have the spirit to fight such a serious illness. There was no way to be sure his body and spirit would cope–or whether the couple looking to adopt him would just move on to another dog.

We needn't have worried. Casper's calvary had arrived. This couple wasn't in search of just any dog; John and Michelle had come specifically for him. They were so in love with Casper that they came to the shelter every day while he was quarantined and sat outside his kennel so they could talk to him through the glass door and keep him company. They couldn't go in, but after their first few visits, he started to look forward to their arrival and would get excited to see them.

On the day his quarantine ended, Casper went home. He went home to more than a new family, he went home to a pack! John and Michelle's three other dogs were led by an elderly Boxer who Casper really bonded with. They nap together, and the whole family goes for long outdoor adventures when the dogs aren't romping around the backyard or cuddling on the couch with Mom and Dad. Casper still suffers from social anxiety, but the

*Casper cuddling his brother, Luca.*

family has been working with him and he's come a long, long way from the frightened Dogo Argentino who wouldn't budge. He's happy, friendly, and he's a pillar of light.

It's worth saying a little more about fear—and what we can do to help dogs even if they make us afraid (whether we admit it or not).

You've probably heard people say that dogs can smell fear. It's true. They can smell when you're afraid, and if you're entering a shelter and you're scared, the dogs will become scared. And that's when a dog's behavior can become unpredictable and sometimes aggressive. (The fact that Casper never became aggressive in the shelter is a testament to what an amazing family member he is going to be!)

If you want to volunteer in a shelter but you're nervous about dogs, don't go in there thinking it's important not to be afraid because you don't want a dog to smell your fear and attack you. I think it's okay to be scared as long as you're open about it and let courage lead the way. Courage isn't an emotion but a choice. Lead with courage, start small (literally with small dogs), and work your way up if you feel comfortable. Think about doing it for the dogs and you'll be more likely to succeed. Dogs can also smell if you're happy, so entering their space on an upbeat note can set the tone for a positive encounter.

Personally, I'd prefer to work with a volunteer who does have some fear of dogs, because they take nothing for granted in the way they approach a strange animal. Dog lovers sometimes make the mistake of believing that loving dogs makes them good with dogs—and that dogs will automatically love them back. No, there's nothing automatic about it. Being more apprehensive often results in people taking the time to learn how to approach a dog properly.

So if you've always wanted to work with dogs, you really can just go to a shelter and offer to volunteer. You can even tell the staff, "I'm scared of dogs but I'd like to learn how to help." They can usually use the extra set of hands, and some shelters will even pair you up with an experienced person who can show you the ropes and help with that anxiety. Maybe they once felt it, too.

Casper with his new dad, John.

*Casper at home snuggling with his mom, Michelle.*

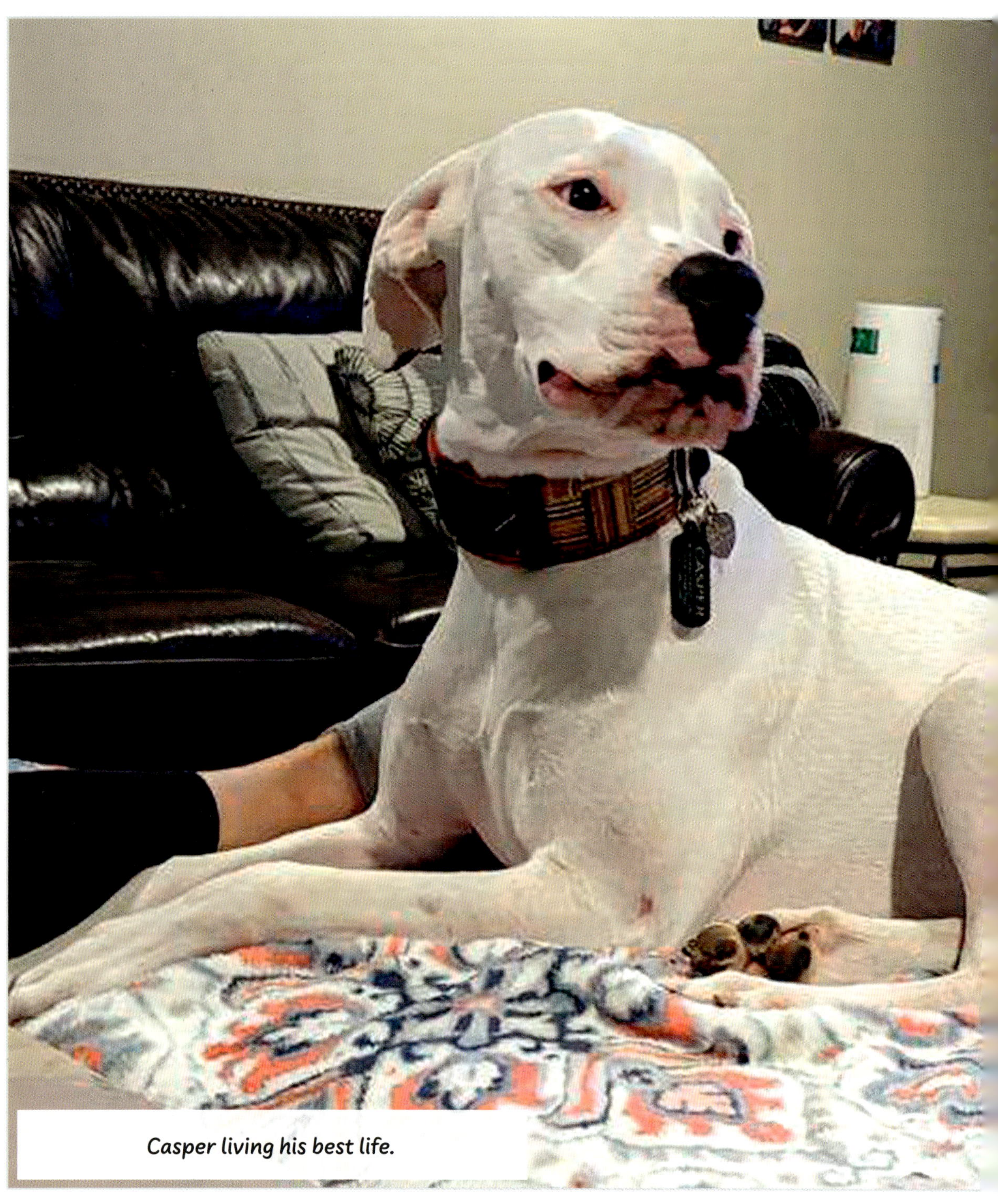

*Casper living his best life.*

You don't need to start with Great Danes or Pit Bulls. You could offer to spend some time with a Lhasa Apso or Cocker Spaniel (but don't make the mistake of thinking you can take less care to avoid aggression in smaller dogs than big ones).

You wouldn't be on your best behavior if you were locked in a tiny space yourself. As Jennifer said to me, the dogs didn't ask to be there, so we shouldn't blame them for acting like they wished they were somewhere else. But if we acknowledge our fear and take the time to overcome it, then we can make a big difference in these dogs' lives. Maybe even save them.

# CHAPTER 3

# KOBE

# (THE DOG WITH A BROKEN HEART)

SCAN TO LEARN MORE
ABOUT KOBE'S STORY

**You might think there are good times to foster a dog, times when life has left you with a little extra space in your life and love to give. And you might think there are bad times, when life is just too busy. Well, during the early months of 2020, Kelly was pregnant, COVID had just shut everything down, and I'd just had heart surgery as a result of my stroke. We were running The Dog Bakery and trying to establish our dog adoption channel online while caring for an aging Boxer whose health would always be compromised by his juvenile case of distemper and a headstrong little terrier. You might think all of those things combined meant that this was one of those bad times to consider fostering a dog.**

Then we met Kobe.

Kobe was a big, floppy, Cane Corso puppy with several special needs. He has taught us many things over the years, but more than anything he reminds us that there's no time like the present to live life to its fullest.

---

Early in the new year, my friend Tye Friis called. Tye was running Reversed Rescue in Leona Valley, California. He specializes in Pit Bulls and other bully breeds. There was a dog he wanted me to meet, but there was a catch.

"I was wondering if you could foster him."

So, yeah, it wasn't the ideal moment for us to add a dog to our household. But one thing I've learned in working with rescue animals is that it's never about whether the time is right for you, it's about whether you can be there for a dog when they need you. And boy, did Kobe need somebody.

Tye had received a call about Kobe from a veterinarian he knows. The vet had a Cane Corso puppy brought in, and his health was a mess. Not only did he appear to be blind, he had serious heart troubles. The vet estimated the puppy had maybe three months to live. His owner was so overwhelmed by his medical issues that he'd tried to return the dog to the breeder. When the breeder refused, the owner brought him to the vet to be euthanized. But the vet hesitated.

The puppy was full of life and not in pain, and he wouldn't be in pain right up to the moment his heart ceased to pump. That could happen any day or a few months down the road, but until then Kobe could live

**Kelly fell in love with Kobe on day one.**

a good life—if Tye was willing to take him off the vet's hands by the end of the day.

Tye's rescue was full, so he called me. Kelly and I talked it over. She was so early in her pregnancy that we hadn't even told people about the baby. Sad as it was to consider, chances were Kobe's heart would fail long before the baby was born. We could give him those few good months in our care.

We agreed. "Let's do it."

~~~

Like any rescue, Tye's was always in need of food and supplies, as well as toys and treats to keep the dogs stimulated. We decided we'd make an adventure out of helping him stock up. We met him and Kobe at a pet store and arranged with the store for Kobe to have the run of the aisles. We'd make a video of it, and Kobe would share the spotlight with a couple of Tye's other rescues, Penelope, a Frenchie who used a wheelchair for her immobile rear legs, and a Pit Bull named Miss Piggy who we'd featured before. She still wasn't adopted, which shocked me because she was so darned cute. (Pitties can be tough to find homes for, as there are a lot of undeserved stereotypes about them that have resulted in difficulties with landlords and even home insurers. But in my opinion that bad rap is totally undeserved.) Everything the three dogs touched as they tore around the shop, we would buy for Tye's rescue.

The dogs spent nearly a thousand bucks, but the real lasting impact of that day for Kelly and me was meeting this cuddly Cane Corso. Everything about him made us want to pick him up. He was only a few months old, but Kelly had to put her entire might into lifting him. With his big floppy ears, he was a real-life Dumbo out of the Disney story, and he had the most expressive dog eyes I'd ever seen. They caught your attention and just captivated you.

That might seem odd to say about the eyes of an apparently blind puppy, but Kobe's eyes weren't cloudy or misdirected. They followed you around like you'd expect from a dog who was watching you and seemed to do everything right—except see.

As we encouraged Kobe to try treats and play with toys, he sniffed his way around with real excitement, loving the plushy stuff against his nose and getting into a standoff with a tough chew-rope that didn't feel so great when he bumped into it. I was totally won over by his
~~~

willingness to explore. Kelly and I were both falling head over heels in love with him.

Kobe was amazing, but he sometimes got a little overwhelmed. So we'd stop, but then he'd want to get back on the floor to keep exploring toys and treats. A few times he batted at them with his paw and then jumped back, to see if he had just found something that would play with him. He expressed so much emotion with his eyes, we figured he must be able to see light and shadow, at least.

Before long, he was slowing down. He couldn't run around, obviously, because he couldn't navigate the aisles visually, but he also ran out of energy early and ended his day, crashed out happily in a baby buggy for dogs.

March 2020 brought another complication in Kobe's life. The pandemic came to California, and suddenly getting an appointment with specialist veterinarians meant long waiting lists. We scheduled appointments for Kobe and did what we could to make the best of it at home with him, Flip, and Zoey, our terrier. We made great meals for him, and he got to play with the other dogs. Flip was his usual great self. He really shone in those moments. This oversized puppy shows up out of nowhere, and he acts weird, running into things and not reacting when other dogs approach. Flip just rolled with the change.

Zoey was a different story. Small, senior, and scrappy, when she marched through the room, she expected everyone to get out of her way. Kobe wouldn't move. He had no way to know she was coming until he felt her bump into him or got close enough that he smelled her. And he didn't know to make the subtle signs of subservience that she expected, like tail tucking. He would jump out of the way when she collided with him, surprised and a little bit afraid. Flip was always patient with him when he was feeling scorned.

When we finally got Kobe in to see a cardiology specialist, he confirmed that Kobe had tricuspid valve disease and pulmonary stenosis. In short, one side of his heart worked and the other didn't. His heart would receive blood on one side, then pump it to the other side, where nothing would happen. One side of his heart was doing all the work of pumping blood through his body. Strictly speaking, half of

Kobe's heart was already in failure, and complete failure was inevitable, especially given how big that Cane Corso body would eventually grow. The specialist's direction was simple: Make him comfortable and let him enjoy the time he has.

Stubbornness isn't always a bad thing. We wanted to know whether Kobe had any chance of living a longer life. "What," I asked the vet, "would a procedure to help Kobe look like, if such a procedure existed?" I'm glad I persisted because such a procedure did exist, it just had a very low chance of success and would be very expensive. And we couldn't even think about it until Kobe's heart grew larger–if he survived long enough for that to happen.

We went home and put our minds to how we could make this procedure possible. We were just fostering Kobe, meaning he was still legally in the care of Reversed Rescue. So we held a fundraiser online and said we would match money raised to pay for Kobe's operation. We were clear that the operation wasn't sure to succeed, because the specialist had been careful to manage our expectations. But hope is a powerful motivator. People responded. They were as in love with Kobe as we were, and the

Baby Kobe exploring our backyard for the first tin

donations soon added up to our target amount.

In the meantime, we still wanted to know if we could help Kobe's eyesight. We were excited when the date for his appointment finally came up. We were so sure his sight could be recovered, given the way his eyes followed us around. We were wrong. The ophthalmologist took one look at Kobe and said he would never be able to see.

Kobe's health always struck me as a symptom of what goes wrong when backyard breeders are in business just to make an easy buck. The mothers have too many litters, and the puppies are often inbred. Whatever it takes to pump out more expensive dogs with no regard for their health. Kobe was born with neurological issues. His paws tremble, for instance. And then we learned his optic nerve didn't work. His eyeballs worked and looked fine from the outside, but his condition—optic nerve hypoplasia—means the nerve that should communicate images to his brain had not developed. Kobe was permanently 100 percent blind.

I'd be lying if I said the news didn't disappoint me. I hid it from everyone, including Kobe, but it set me back for a day or two. I soon rallied and focused on our goal: making sure Kobe's short life was amazing. There was another obstacle to that, however. His anxiety levels were really high. His heart beat extra quickly to compensate for its partial failure, which gave Kobe a false sense of anxiety. Imagine drinking too much caffeine and your heart starts going a mile a minute and you feel anxious even though nothing is happening to cause you stress. Kobe was always in that state, so we had to be constantly aware of keeping our own energy from overexciting him.

His heart condition led to another problem. His rapid pulse kept his metabolism running high, plus he was growing quickly. Putting enough weight on him and keeping it on was a constant effort. With most dogs, it's important to be mindful of their calorie intake because they want unlimited treats. But with Kobe it was the exact opposite: We were coming up with creative ways to give him extra calories in as healthy a way as possible.

Fortunately, feeding a cute, giant puppy healthy treats was fun to share with everyone that had fallen in love with him and was following his story on social media. We shared videos of Kobe and Flip trying vegetables and chicken breast

*Kobe, the happy puppy.*

***Flip being patient and guiding a blind and anxious puppy named Kobe.***

(breast only–no bones!), we brewed up homemade puppuccinos with vegan rice whipped cream. It's low in fat, sugar, and sodium, so it's not *too* unhealthy for dogs and is safe as an occasional treat. (You wouldn't let your teenager live on a steady diet of whipped cream, right? But you'd still let them have a little. Well, the same thing goes with dogs, and for the same reasons.) I love to cook for dogs, and Kobe got steak and my special dog food mix of veggies, rice, and blueberries, which he devoured. With most dogs, being mindful of calories is important, because they will take treats all day, every day! But with Kobe, the goal was to get as many healthy calories into him as possible.

The time we spent waiting for our next appointment with the cardiologist gave us a chance to learn all the ways Kobe's condition affected his behavior. I'd noticed how floppy he was when we first met him at the pet store. He was doing something I call "pancaking." When he was unsure what to do, because he couldn't take visual cues from the other dogs, he'd flop on the floor and wait for direction from me. I'd let him know I was there by gently booping (bumping) his nose with my hand so he could smell me and know he was safe. Even something as unthreatening as a new treat could make him anxious, so we'd put him at ease, take it slow, and let him follow my lead or Flip's as much as he could.

I used treats to teach him to sit, which he learned quickly even though he often sat facing away from me. Much harder for him was climbing stairs. And going down stairs was extra scary. You try doing that with your eyes closed. (Or maybe don't!) Stairs are intimidating when you can't see the steps.

Unfortunately, after a few happy months with Kobe had gone by, we were seeing signs of trouble. He was breathing heavily and didn't have much energy. Our fundraising had gone well, though, so we talked to the specialist again and asked if he'd be willing to try the surgery. To our surprise, he said yes. He'd been very upfront about the high cost and low probability of success since most people aren't in a position to pay for such an expensive operation, and veterinarians are sensitive to people's budgets (even if their bills don't always reflect that sensitivity!) But with our fundraising for Tye's rescue and my matching the total, we had raised what we needed. And more importantly, we believed in Kobe. We just could not imagine not trying whatever might give him the longest, happiest life possible.

We scheduled a visit with the specialist for the next day, but soon we weren't sure we could wait even a single night. The day was a hot one, and Kobe was really laboring. He was resting his head constantly—on an ottoman, on our laps—and breathing fast.

I had an idea. With Kobe's surgery pending and less-than-great odds that he'd survive, I told Kelly I wanted to surprise Kobe with a basketful of toys, plush ones, the kind that he loves to press his nose against. We put a blanket down in the backyard and got out the camera to share some videos with Kobe's fans. Kelly was much further along in her pregnancy by this time, so it was all kinds of awkward and fun. I dumped the toys, Kobe went nuts, and then I handed Kelly some papers—adoption papers.

We had promised ourselves when we started fostering dogs that we wouldn't adopt them. We can handle only so many animals at once, and if we adopt the ones that are doing well, we forfeit the opportunity to foster dogs who really need us. By making that promise to each other, it prevents us from giving in when we've fallen in love with a foster dog. But with Kelly being pregnant, and Kobe being such a cuddlebug, she couldn't let him go. Neither could I.

As much as we loved Kobe, there was more to breaking our promise than just wanting to keep him. The shock of going to a new family and a new home could be more than Kobe's heart could handle. Losing the companionship of Flip, or maybe sharing a strange home with a new dog who could be even more of a bully than little Zoey would be too much. If the surgery worked for him and extended his life, he would be here to stay. And if he didn't make it through the surgery, which was likely, he would leave this world as a part of our family, as Kobe Kanaka. And I think in his way he knew it.

Tears followed. And a lot of joy. But as the day moved into evening, we became fixated watching him, watching his ribs go up and down at an alarming pace. It got worse overnight, so much so that by morning on the day of the appointment he couldn't lift his head at all. We didn't wait for our scheduled time. I lifted him into the truck and we rushed to the clinic. He was so fatigued, the staff had to roll him in on a gurney.

That's when Kobe's heart stopped. I stood inside the clinic lobby, watching as the staff pounded on

*Kobe learning to trust me on a walk.*

*Kobe going to the emergency room.*

his chest, trying to bring him back to life. I hated being even this far from him at that moment; he should have spent his final moments in our arms, knowing he was loved. We hadn't brought him this far only to pass in the hands of strangers. And then, relief among the staff. Kobe was breathing again.

The specialist was already at the clinic. The workup he had planned for Kobe, to determine whether he was a good candidate for the surgery, was no longer an option. He would have to begin emergency surgery while we hoped and prayed for no complications. Anesthesia alone can be more than a weak heart can handle. We spent nine hours on pins and needles before the specialist called us. We couldn't meet in person because we were still in the heaviest time of COVID lockdowns.

"I have news," he said. Not good or bad news, just news. The surgery was complete, and Kobe was doing well, he told us. But only time would tell if the procedure had actually worked.

Days later we were able to take him home. About a week after his recovery, Kobe was right back to his old self, which was perfect timing, because Kelly had just given birth to our daughter, Capri.

We had six months. That was the cardiologist's best guess. Cane Corsos are very big dogs; they grow as large as 150 pounds. The strength of Kobe's heart probably wouldn't keep up with that kind of growth. So we set our minds back to where we had started: making every day with Kobe a great day for him and us.

Managing his excitement was a tightrope walk. He was taking several medications, some of which would make him super thirsty and lead him to drink excessively. Some would make him lose his appetite, which we would try to stimulate with flavors like cinnamon. Then, as soon as we struck the right balance, his tastes would change. We realized at one point that he loved salmon, so we stocked the freezer with it. Next thing we knew he was turning his nose up at fish. That constant game became a vicious cycle because when Kobe slowed his eating, his medication dosages would fall out of alignment with his body weight, which was fluctuating. Fluid would fill his lungs, he'd stop eating altogether, and we'd find ourselves in dangerous territory.

Our vet bills skyrocketed. I'd never taken a dog to see the vet as often as I took Kobe. But we were quick studies in what nutrition and hydration do to a dog's body, and we managed to fix every imbalance until, before we knew it, we had reached six months. And he was still waking up happy every day, ready for whatever adventure we could think of.

Another six months passed. Kobe was now as big as Flip, and the specialist told us his heart had actually been growing and the walls of his heart had been getting thicker. We got to four years old and the specialist could only look on in amazement.

"Have you ever seen anything like this?" I asked him.

"Absolutely not," he replied. Never in all his years of practice had he seen a dog outlive such dismal odds.

What do you think?" I pressed. "How much longer do you think he has to live? Five?"

He thought about it. "Five...?"

"Great. So we have another year with him?"

To my surprise, he said, "No, not that he'll live to five years old, I think he'll live another five years."

Kobe has learned a lot since then. His ears and nose have always been super sensitive. He is the first one to hear a cat outside or a coyote. And sneaking a snack in the kitchen without him noticing–forget it! But it's how his nose allows him to map out space that is so incredible–more specifically, how his whiskers do.

You've probably noticed big whiskers on a cat, but I didn't know how important whiskers are for a dog until I watched Kobe learn to navigate our house. I worried that he would run into things constantly, like he did as a puppy, but he doesn't. When he approaches a corner, he seems like he is going to run right into the wall. He gets so close to it that I want to call, "Look out!" But then he just grazes the corner, like he knew it was there all along. It's his whiskers telling him where the wall is, and Cane Corsos have some big whiskers, thankfully. In fact, his whiskers don't even need to touch the wall. Static electricity alerts him to objects before he even makes contact. If someone who didn't know he was blind came to our house, Kobe navigates the space so effectively that they'd never know he was blind.

Family picture with our first daughter along with Kobe, Flip, and Zoey.

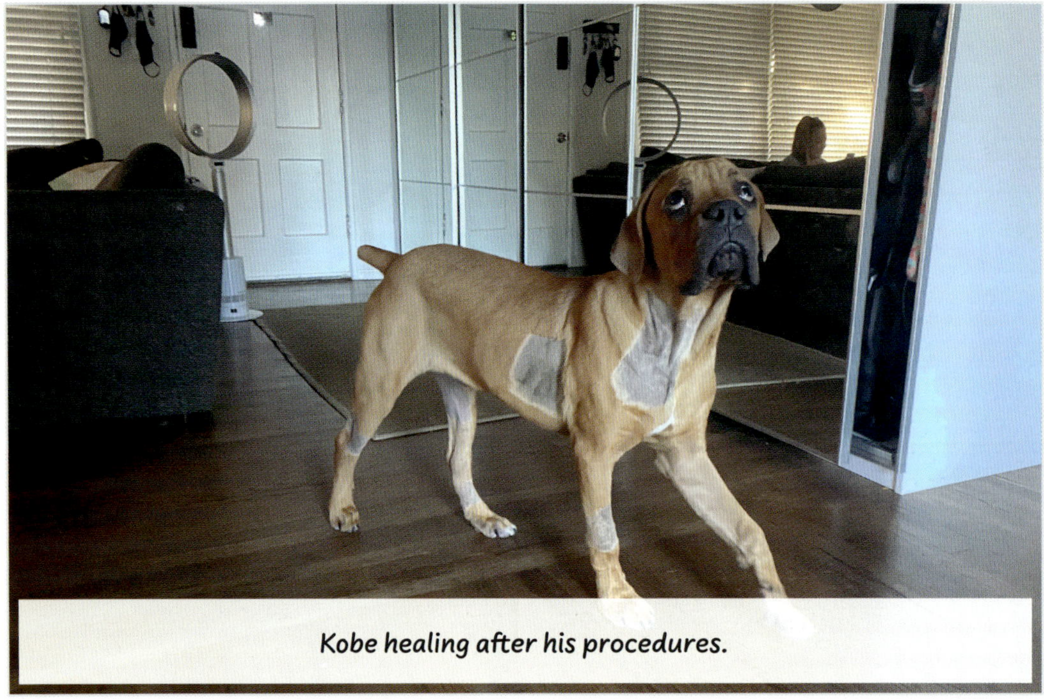
Kobe healing after his procedures.

By the time you're reading this, Kobe will be five years old. That was unimaginable when we met him. Still, we have to remind ourselves that Kobe won't be with us forever, or for as long as most dogs are, anyway. Sure, he's had some luck. His whole life hung on a coincidence when his owner took him to a vet who had second thoughts about euthanizing an animal that was so happy to be alive, and who happened to know a rescue operator who knew someone who could foster a puppy on a few hours' notice. And all of this just a month before COVID quarantine would have made this lucky sequence of events nearly impossible. But in the five years since Kobe's fateful day, the blessing has been all ours.

In my early days with Kobe, I saw the effect on his anxiety when I just sat with him to help him calm down. After a heart surgery related to my stroke, I wore a heart monitor for a while. I have a really healthy heart rate from running, but getting down on the floor with Kobe made even my heart rate slow down. In fact, sitting like that with my dogs serves as a constant reminder of the positive impact a few minutes of low-key time together can have on me and any dog I sit with. So thanks to Kobe for that, too.

Kobe looking handsome in his bow tie.

Our kiddos with Kobe on Christmas.

Because of his anxiety, we've never enrolled Kobe in formal dog training. The pressure on dogs in training is more than we figured his heart could take. And he's already tuned in to what we want from him because he relies on us to direct him more than other dogs would. As a result, the need for training was never very pronounced with him. But now? He's taking less medication. He's over a hundred pounds, though we still have to watch that his weight doesn't slip. He has kidney issues, and his heart will always work overtime. But he seems more durable than ever, enough so that training is a real consideration, as are more stimulating adventures, like visiting the beach and letting him splash in the ocean waves.

He's always ready to experience new things, even if it's stressful. The way he navigates life is astonishing. Any day that we haven't lived up to the opportunity he gives us only makes us say, "Tomorrow we'll try harder." We became parents shortly after Kobe arrived, and it's hard to imagine a better lesson or a more fortunate time to learn it.

Kobe is a testament to everything that makes dogs such great additions to our families. He wakes up every day with excitement and joy in his heart. We can see it in his eyes, even if they can't see us back. Some dogs give you those cute eyes very strategically, trying to get a treat or extra attention. Kobe just shows his true self all the time, because he doesn't know we can see him. He doesn't realize that the rest of his family can see! He just thinks we're all navigating like he does, and we're all in this together.

Whenever things go wrong in life, it can hold you back. Things go wrong for Kobe every day. They never keep him down. He just shakes it off and pushes forward. We should all take a lesson from him. You think people can see scars and war wounds on you from all your mistakes. Kobe reminds us they can't. I've learned from him that it's not always others seeing our weaknesses and judging us for them—it's often us, holding ourselves back.

Whether we have another year with Kobe or another five, we'll be lucky to have that time. So long as we have him, we have to work really hard to return that blessing to him.

For now, we aren't incorporating any foster or farm dogs with Kobe. We tried for a few months with a little French Bulldog mix named Tulip who was rehabilitating from hip surgery, but she responded to his unusual behavior just like Zoey did. So we have accepted that it's okay to focus on the one dog who really needs us. Sooner or later, the day will come when we pay the blessing of Kobe forward to other dogs we meet.

And along the way, we'll take it slow and share our journey with this incredible Cane Corso who teaches us so much about living and loving each day, even with a broken heart.

*On Flip Farms with Kobe at the newly built rescue Quonset hut.*

# CHAPTER 4

# MACY

## (GETTING THROUGH THIS TOGETHER)

SCAN TO LEARN MORE
ABOUT MACY'S STORY

**We don't always know what dogs have experienced before they arrive in a shelter. Sometimes they endure negligence, sometimes cruelty, or sometimes an owner just doesn't have the ability to care for a dog properly but has been hesitant to give it up. Whatever the story, it's when I meet a dog who has been through the worst that I'm often reminded of the best reasons we love dogs.**

Starved and wasting away when she was left in night drop, a German Shepherd we nicknamed Macy had every reason not to trust people, especially the guy inching his way into her kennel the morning after she arrived at the shelter. But she didn't growl or hide from me. She was nervous and scared, sure. But her profound need for affection and her determination to love—two feelings she clearly hadn't enjoyed much of in her life—led us to develop a powerful bond.

Whenever I arrive at a shelter, I walk up and down the kennel rows. Some of the dogs are curious when I pass, and they step up to the door of their kennel to check me out. I'd love to spend time with them, but they're already showing that they've got what it takes to charm potential adopters.

I'm looking for the dogs who are going to need some extra attention to get them up on their feet and show people how wonderful they would be to take home. I'm also looking for the ones in such dire health they might not survive without the kind of extra care and emotional lift that shelters don't often have the time or budget to provide.

Each shelter and rescue is set up differently, but most have a lot in common. The shelter in Southern California where I spend a lot of my time has a sally port area, where dogs are delivered by animal control; reception, where they're surrendered to the shelter's care; and a night drop. When dogs come in through those areas the staff checks them in, and then they typically move to health check to assess whether the dog can be put in general population. Some dogs that have serious medical needs are brought directly to a medical hold area, a space out of view of the public, where dogs stay while the next steps are decided.

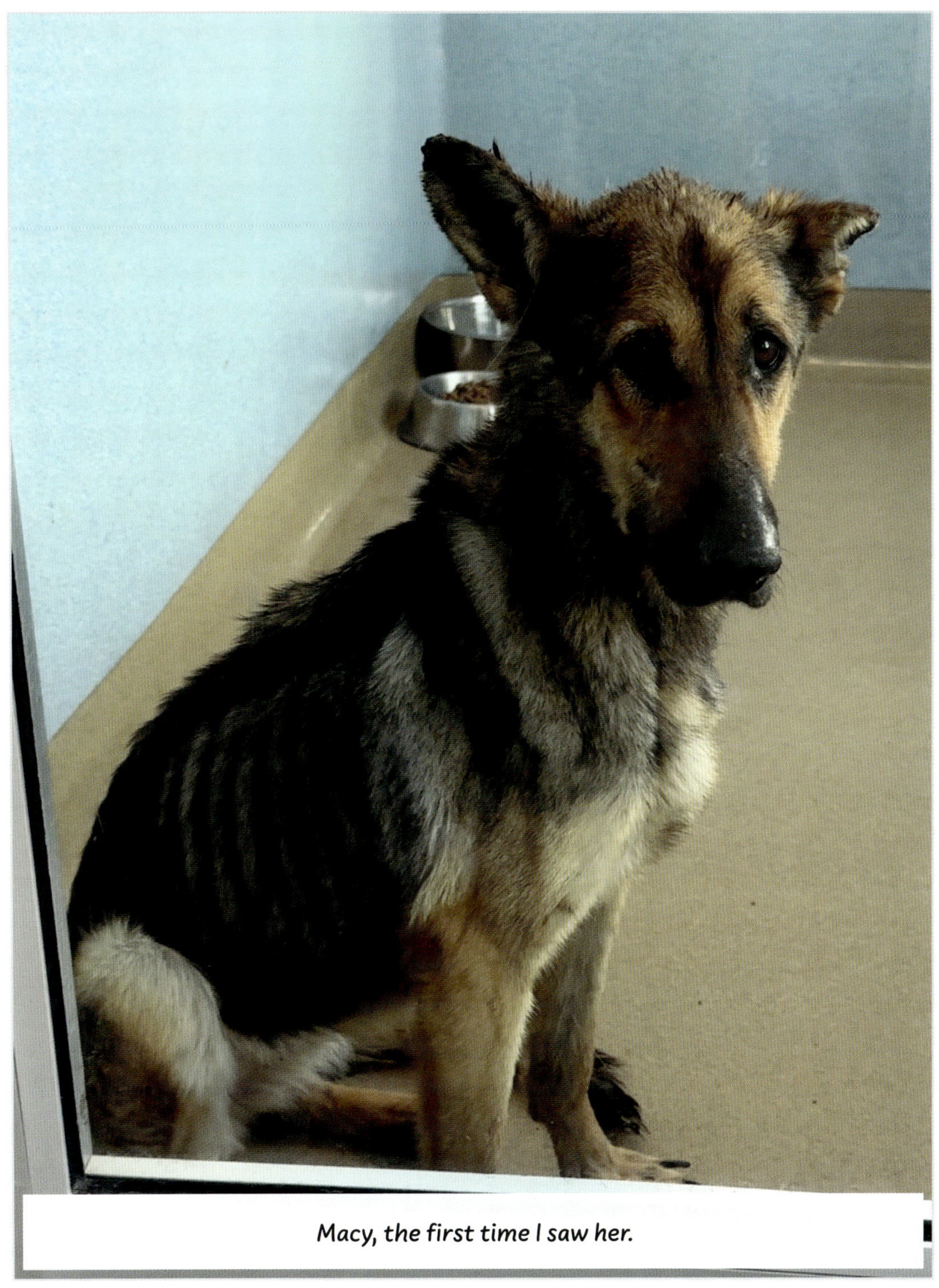

*Macy, the first time I saw her.*

Some of those dogs have arrived injured and in need of vet care. Sometimes they're involved in a legal case, because Animal Control witnessed abuse of the dog or has other reasons to believe cruelty was involved. One of the worst signs of abuse is starvation. I can't imagine why anyone allows a dog to starve, but I've seen it more times than I'll ever forget. And one of the worst cases was waiting for me that morning.

The sight of this German Shepherd hit me hard. She was in a nice kennel, a large one with blankets and food and water. She had been brought in only hours before I got there. She was filthy dirty. And skinny. So skinny it hurt just to look at her. Every rib was sticking out. Her hip bones were plainly visible. There are skinny dogs, then there are starved skinny dogs, and then there's emaciated. This poor girl was emaciated.

The color had left her, which seems like a strange thing to say about an animal with a colorful coat. But she'd lost the luster that gives a healthy dog its beauty. To see a dog that has lost that vibrance–it's haunting. She had a large scar under her right eye. I could see every divot in her cranium. Her cheeks were indented. The normal dog shape had left her face.

Seeing her in this condition, it was clear she had been severely deprived of nutrition. This was neglect at a level that wasn't going to be fixed by a few big meals and an armload of treats. There was a big job to do here, and no guarantee a dog this far gone could be nursed back to health.

As I stepped into her kennel, she cowered and paced. She was scared. I started with my usual routine, waiting for the dog to come to me. Sometimes this takes fifteen minutes, and sometimes it takes an hour or never happens at all. I could tell she wanted to connect so badly but didn't know how to approach me. She kept slinking close, cowering and whimpering, and looking as if she might roll over and let me scratch her belly. She was getting comfortable, though. This was submission. Her behavior was driven by pure desperation to connect.

She smelled horrible. Her fur was caked in dirt and feces and urine and who knows what else. I noticed she had food and water but wasn't eating, so I pulled out a large jerky stick. I started giving her some, and she did something I hadn't seen

***Macy receiving some much needed love and affection.***

before. She began chomping, at the air, at the treat... at my hand as I gave her the treat! She wasn't being aggressive. She was clearly famished, but she also didn't seem to know how to take food offered by hand.

We went through a bunch of jerky sticks. That hollow sound of her jaws chomping, I can still hear it. It's the sound of starvation, and it's terrible. The shelter had provided kibble, but they hadn't been able to spend enough time with her to realize that the usual food bowl wasn't going to work. A big stainless-steel dish was probably alien to this dog. That's often the case with dogs who have come from hoarding situations or were feral and had never eaten from a bowl. Glimpses of their own movement reflected in the shining metal scare them. Plus, it's just a weird, alien object. I confirmed this suspicion by taking some of the kibble from the bowl and putting it on the blanket. She gobbled it up.

When the shepherd wouldn't calm down, I moved myself to the door. I needed her to stop pacing. Sitting sideways in front of the door made her stop thinking about getting out. Of course she wanted to bolt. In all likelihood, she had never been confined in a space that was actually safe.

Maybe the move worked. Maybe it was the positive affirmations I gave her next. I'm sure she'd never been told she was a "good girl" before–or more to the point, spoken to in a reassuring tone of voice. Within a few moments, she came over, pressed her face against my chest, and tucked her nose under my chin. She licked and sniffed a little, then she started to cry.

The normal dog whimpering had turned quickly into something like a human cry, and I could feel her plea for affection deep in my gut. She didn't have the luxury of playing it safe and instead bet on my careful approach, meaning she could rely on me to not hurt her. I held her head against my chest and felt her feeble neck. I felt something coming from her like gratitude for holding the weight of the head she could barely keep up on her own. If you've ever had a living being press their head against you in such a desperate state, you will never forget it. Time freezes, and the only thing that matters is that moment. You take on all the sorrow and pain as your own and give back all the love and comfort you can.

I just kept thinking, "I've got you. We're going to get through this together." Feeling that from

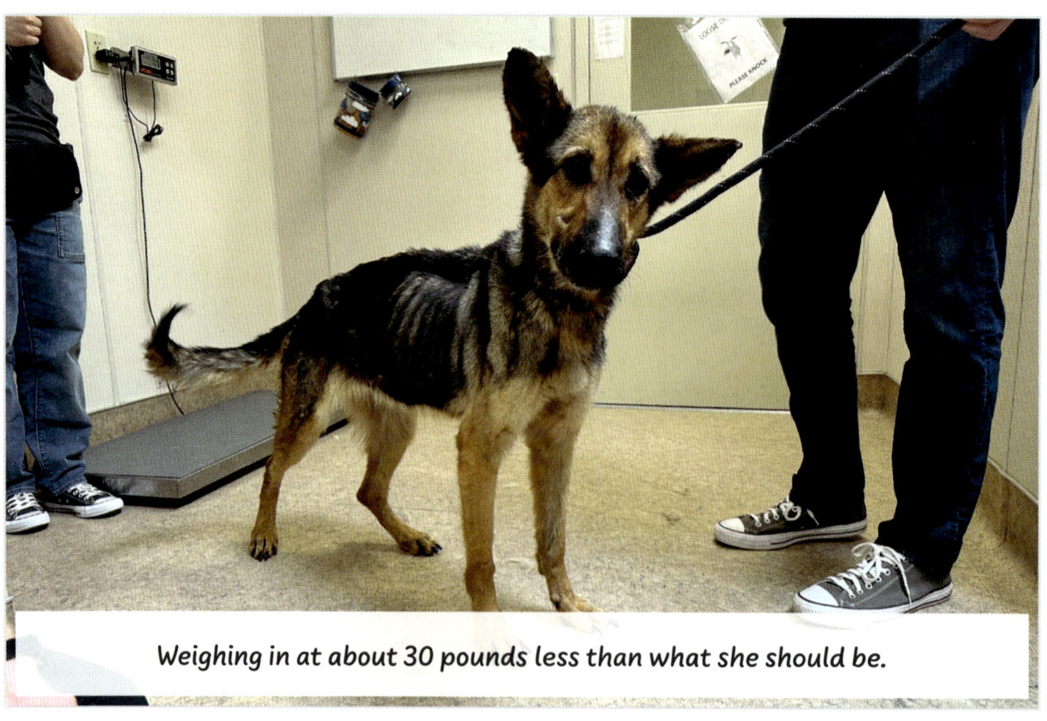

***Weighing in at about 30 pounds less than what she should be.***

another person can make you feel you can get through almost anything. I wanted this poor shepherd to feel it from me.

That moment seemed to last forever. When it finally passed, I was left with an overwhelming sense of anger, sadness, frustration, despair, and disbelief, all at the same time. I often feel this in these situations. I call it the two-minute drop. After I've gathered some information on the dog's situation and the gravity of what they've been through hits me, my heart and stomach sink and my anger rises.

There's a way out of this feeling. First, I focus on hitting the mute button on the noise. The anger doesn't go away exactly, but I try to silence it in my mind. Then I remind myself that this dog has probably now been through the hardest part: the neglect or abuse; being abandoned or given up then caught on the street by Animal Control or a stranger, or maybe being brought here by an owner who can't keep them, for reasons the dog can't understand; then landing in a shelter full of other frightened dogs, with all the barking and whining going on around them. It's a terrifying journey. But they're here now, in a secure building, and they have food and water, and no coyotes are following them; there are no cars to dodge as they scrounge for food. They get cleaned up and checked by a vet. The staff have limited time to spend with each dog, but they fill that time with all the love and compassion they can offer. For most dogs, the shelter is a corner turned, even if they don't know it yet.

And then I fast forward to several months from now. Adopted, maybe given a new name, the dog has a bright future waiting for her. I think about the things that make dogs dogs, and humans human, and about that rare bond that forms between our species. I think about all the fun mistakes waiting for her, like getting in trouble for sneaking the leftover bagel off the kitchen counter or slipping onto the bed even though she's not supposed to. I think about this girl one day going on walks, with that beautiful German Shepherd posture, her hip slightly sloped down and her ears and snout up.

There might be some training and medical care to get through before that future happens, but

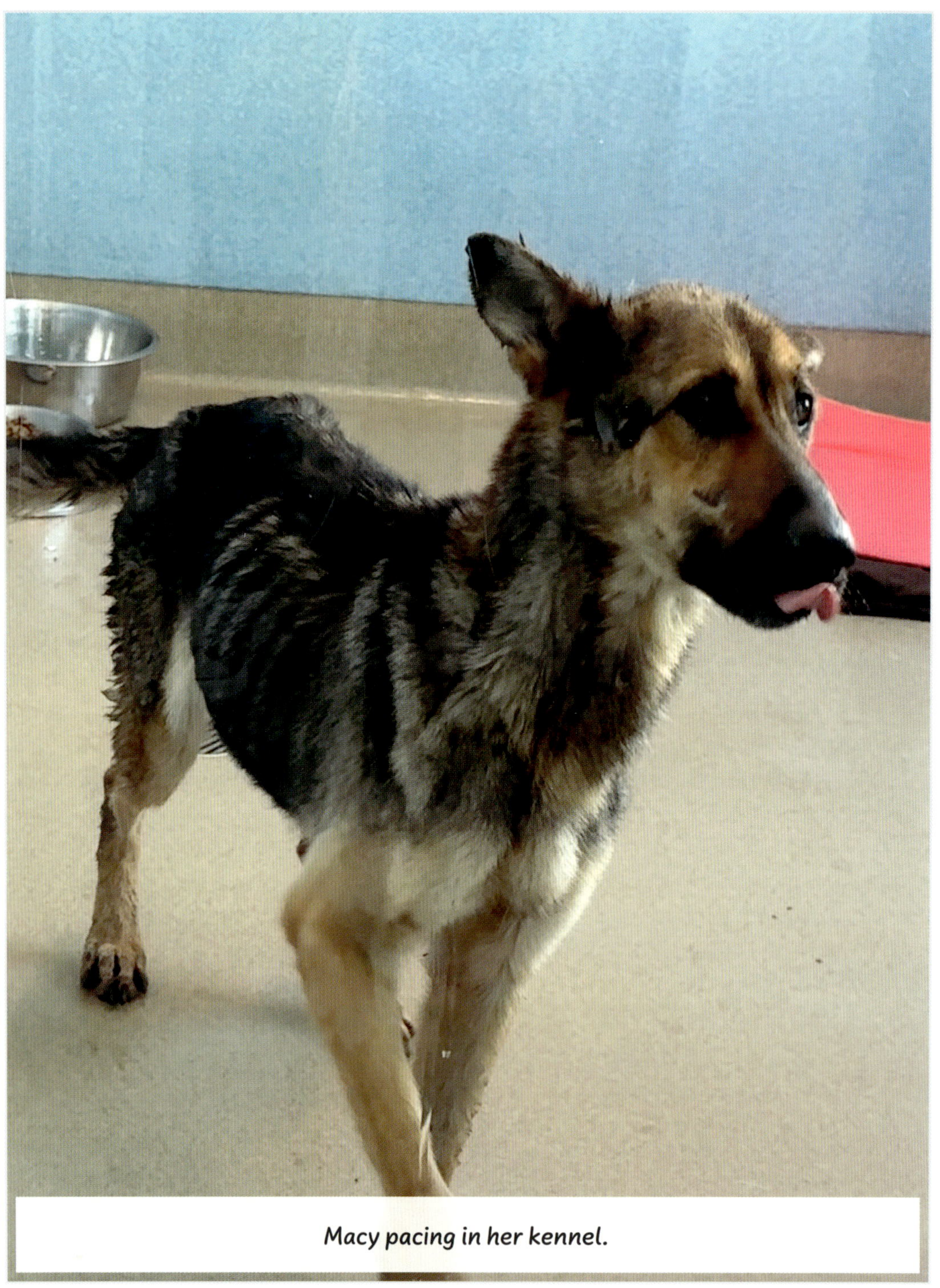

*Macy pacing in her kennel.*

the terrible stuff is done. That's what I think about in those moments when sadness and anger threaten to overwhelm me. And the dogs feel that positivity. It's the attitude they need me to hold on to.

After the emaciated shepherd had spent some time cuddling, she ended her crying and got a drink of water—which was a relief to see her do—and settled on her blankets, calmer now.

I looked for the positive in her health, too. There are reasons other than neglect that can cause a dog to become as skinny as this girl. Cancer thrives in the absence of nourishment. If not cared for properly, an overactive thyroid can leave an animal emaciated like this. And there was no reason yet to think that she didn't have a medical condition *in addition to* being neglected. But she had grabbed those treats out of my hand as quickly as I could produce them. She wouldn't do that if cancer had destroyed her appetite, so that was a positive.

It was time to up my game. We'd brought some Christmas-themed peanut butter cups to the shelter, and I offered her one. It didn't last long. She went through a package so quickly I teared up, and it wasn't from getting my fingers chomped.

I don't always bring fresh-baked treats to the shelter, but I had just happened to on this visit. Baking the goods we produce at The Dog Bakery is cathartic and something I have always done to express my gratitude to dogs. I really do bake love into these treats. So to see her enjoy those so much filled my heart with joy. My only regret was not bringing every treat in my bakery that day—I would have given her every last one of them!

Seriously, though, it's tempting when you see an emaciated dog to think you just need to feed them back to health. But it isn't so simple. A starving dog's organs aren't in a condition to handle that much food; they may even be in organ failure. Food can cause the dog to bloat and their digestive tract to get backed up. Their bodies can't process it. They need frequent small meals of highly nutritious food, with new things introduced only gradually. And even then, the damage to their internal organs might be so severe that there's no recovering. This German Shepherd didn't become emaciated because of a few missed meals. To be like this, she had to starve over time, and if she was going to make it out of this alive, the damage would have to be undone over time as well.

I called a dog rescue group I knew that I thought would be perfect for her. It was clear she was going to need constant attention. I give people who foster dogs all the credit in the world for giving shelter dogs time to find the right family and maybe even recover from medical conditions, but this girl's medical needs were going to be greater than a foster could provide. Unfortunately, the rescue had no space. I could only hope health-check wouldn't find anything wrong with her, beyond the obvious.

Possible ulcer on right eye. Scar on right cheek. Fractured upper canines on both sides of her mouth. Badly worn molars. Pulp exposure on her bottom right incisor. Fly strikes on both ears. Callus sores. Her ears were full of dirt. And it didn't seem to matter which way the staff tried to turn her for examination, the contact caused her discomfort.

Our girl was in rough shape, but nothing so far that couldn't be treated.

It was time to see if she had been spayed, but she wasn't about to trust a stranger to check her out. They asked if I could help, so I got down on the floor and scooped her onto my lap. I couldn't believe how light she was. My heart broke again from her whining and crying. It was a mix of scared, hurt, and relieved, like a child crying after being reunited with a lost parent.

The vet assistant trimmed her belly fur to get a look. No sutures, no scar, no tattoo to indicate that she'd been spayed. So she had at least one operation in her near future. But for all the shepherd's issues, there was no sign of a major condition that would prevent her recovery. Her most serious issue was that she weighed 42 pounds. She should have weighed almost twice that much. But another discovery to come would reveal just how bad her overall health really was.

After health-check, I begged the shelter groomer to squeeze her in for clean up. You might assume shelters automatically clean up strays, but most don't have enough volunteers or budget to groom every animal that comes in. Thankfully, Mel the groomer was always in on Mondays, and when she saw the shepherd, she wanted to help as much as I did.

As it turned out, this would be a sweet moment. Our girl was about to get a name.

*Helping her through her vet checkup.*

I hoisted the shepherd into the groomer's big stainless-steel wash basin. Soon, Mel had her rinsed and covered in soap suds. I left the room for a few minutes to let Mel do her thing, and when I returned she was rinsing the hair on the top of the dog's head. She called me over to show me something. Normally the fur would flatten under the weight of the water. Not this dog's. It stayed sticking up, a sign of dehydration.

The dog was nervous but didn't fight to get out of the tub. I give Mel credit there. She spoke comfortingly to the shepherd and put her at ease. She put medicinal shampoo all over the dog and massaged it in, as her bony joints had barely any skin left from rubbing against whatever hard surfaces she'd been sleeping on. Mel put medicated ointment on her ears, which were sore from flies chewing on them. Flies really plague a dog in this condition, and Mel told me she had seen dogs with half their ears chewed off. The flies, she said, were "attracted to blood like meat on a barbecue." They'd been eating at sores on the shepherd's legs, too.

Medicated from head to toe, the dog got a blow-dry and she looked a bit healthier, and even a little less skinny. She had something else now, too: Mel had decided she'd call her Macy.

Now, a name given in the shelter or at a rescue is really a nickname, a placeholder until a dog is adopted. Sometimes a nickname sticks and sometimes a family gives a dog a new name, one that's meaningful to them. But Macy would do for the moment. Some people have asked me whether "Macy" was short for "emaciated," which would be a pretty terrible name for anyone. No, Mel had been Christmas shopping at Macy's department store and thought it was pretty fancy, and giving Macy this name was Mel's wish for fancy and wonderful things in this dog's future. For everything this dog had lived through, the hope reflected in that name was perfect.

Macy wasn't done, however. She needed her nails trimmed; they had grown far too long. As the staff was clipping them, they were shocked. Macy's nails were incredibly soft. You could have cut through them with a dull knife. The lack of nutrition that had caused this was probably also what had caused her teeth to become so soft that they could wear down as much as they had. It was becoming clear just how deeply malnourishment had affected Macy's entire body.

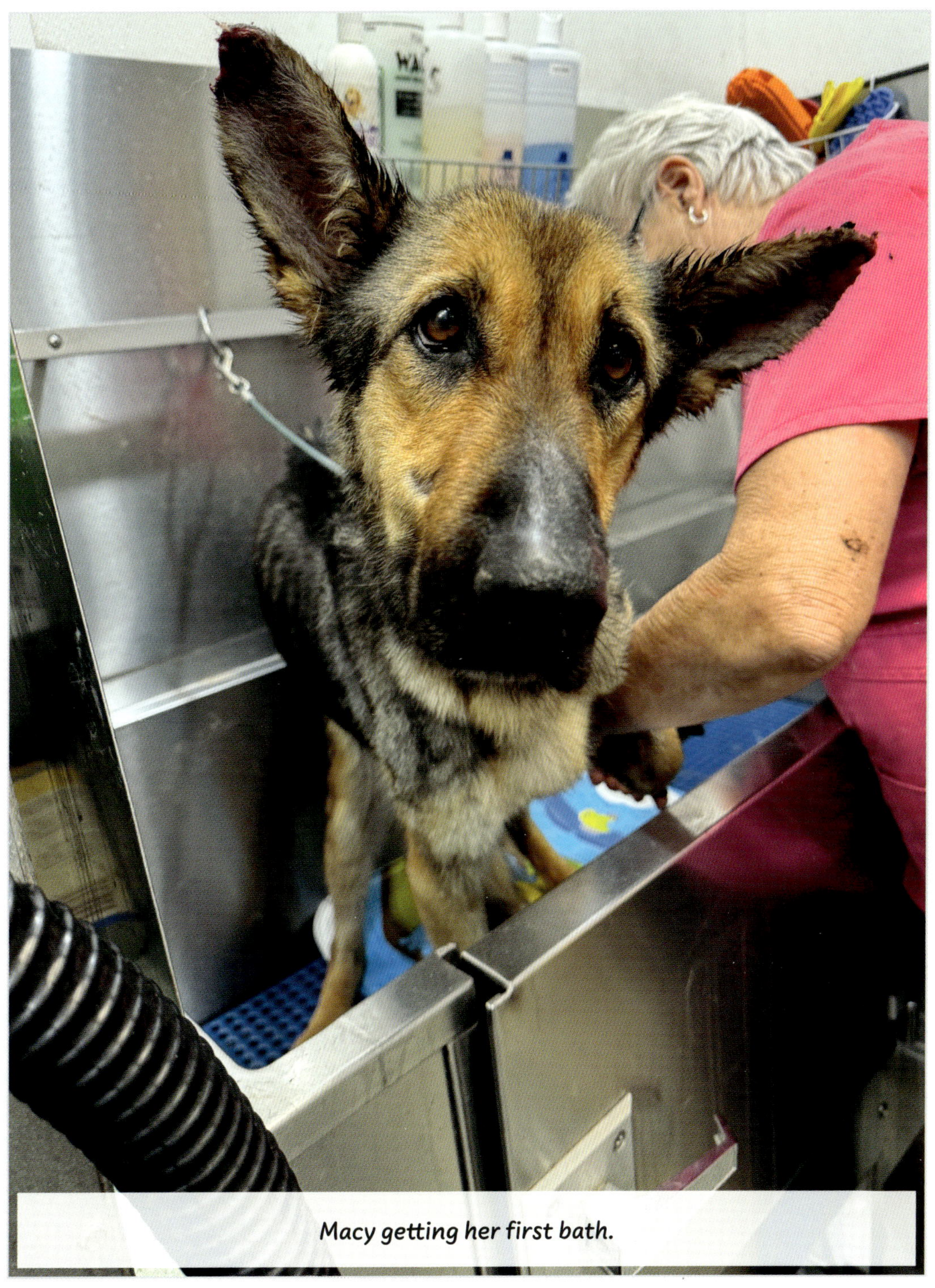

Macy getting her first bath.

Macy needed a plan–a really good plan. And staying at the shelter wasn't it. When shelters receive a dog in Macy's condition, as sad as it is, they often euthanize. Resources are scarce in shelters, and the money it would take to bring a dog in this condition back to good health would be enough to care for several other dogs instead. And Macy was going to need daily intensive care. On top of that, we still didn't know for sure that her weight loss wasn't caused by a serious illness that a quick health check couldn't detect.

Even though I struck out getting Macy into a rescue group, I knew of a veterinary facility about a half-hour outside of Los Angeles that could board Macy and give her the ongoing veterinary attention she needed. I couldn't take her home because Kobe couldn't handle the extra dog in his space.

I probably didn't give the next step enough thought and didn't plan nearly enough, but the bond I had with Macy was now one that could never be broken. I decided to adopt her. Not forever. We would find her a forever home once she was healthy enough. But because I didn't run a nonprofit rescue, in order to take her from the shelter legally I'd need to adopt her. So that's what I did.

First stop in Macy's new life: Norco, California.

Even though Macy was safe, she wasn't saved.

Regulations at the shelter mandate a five-day holding period, during which owners can claim their animals. Had Macy's owners shown up, they could have been charged because of her condition, so it was unlikely we'd see them. But we didn't need trouble down the line because we hadn't followed the rules. And anyway, she needed food and rest to be in any kind of shape for the half-hour drive to Norco.

As soon as Macy was free to go, we got in the truck and headed to Animal Care Services, where the staff put her on fluids and an immediate regimen of small, high-nutrition meals. She also got a nutrient pack (a fluid injection to give her much needed hydration and electrolytes) to help give her body everything it so badly needed. The best news came from the scales. Macy had already put on seven pounds!

My first look at the facility felt good. It was very thoughtfully laid out, with a big window in Macy's kennel making it feel like a room at a

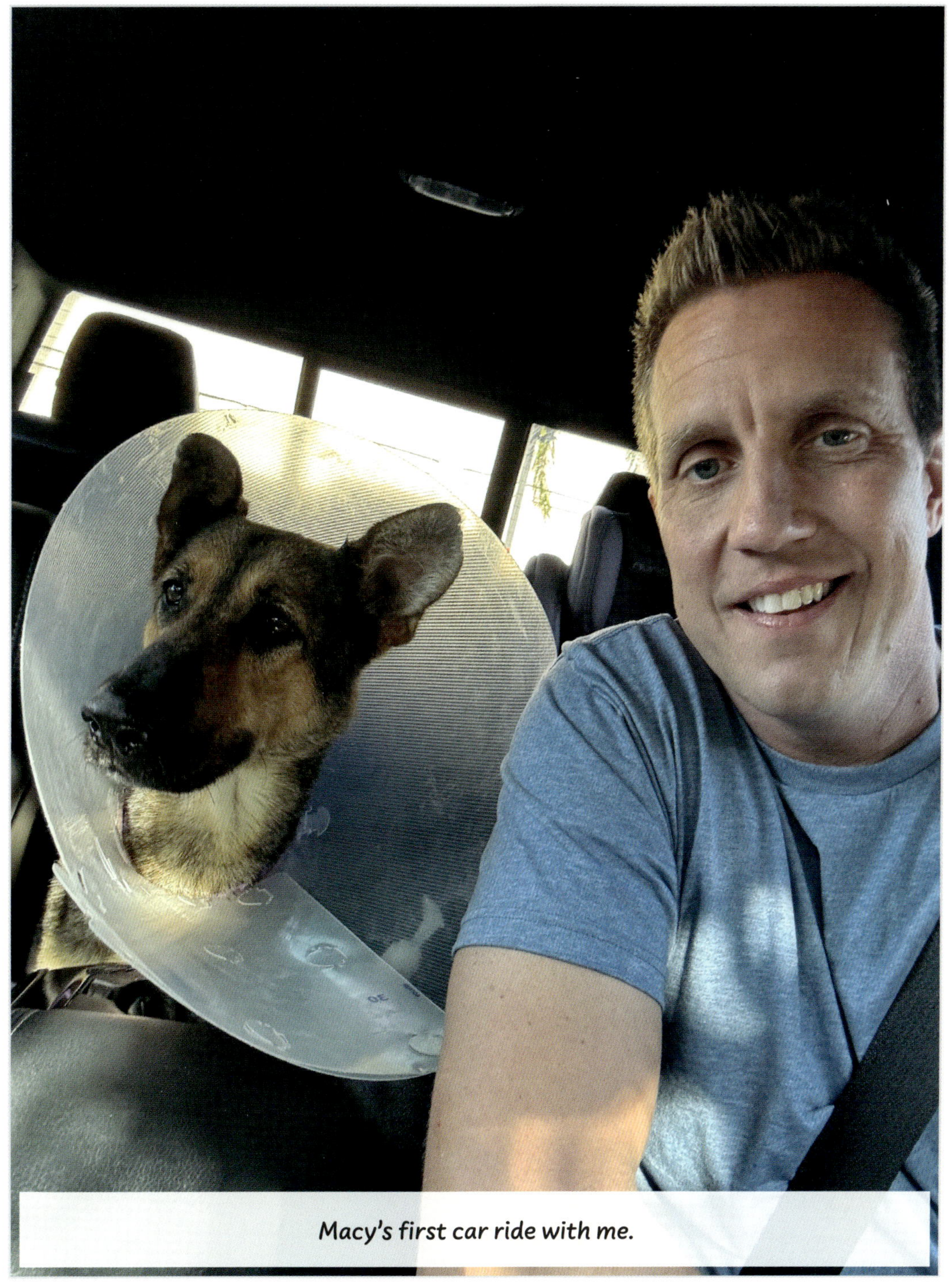

*Macy's first car ride with me.*

dog resort. Animal sculptures decorated the halls, and everything felt brand new. I could tell this place was built with a love of animals in mind.

The plan was for Macy to stay as long as needed to keep putting on weight, work on her behavior, and get her in good condition to be adopted. I left her that first day feeling reassured by the plan but still sad for Macy. She whimpered as I said goodbye. There's just no way to make a dog understand that she really needs to stay behind and that you'll be back regularly to check up on her.

It wasn't long before my phone rang. The vet had discovered an obstruction of some sort in Macy's digestive tract, but because she was still so anxious about sitting still, they couldn't get a clear X-ray to confirm what it was. Starving dogs can eat all kinds of things, and some of those things, like pieces of fabric or rocks, can wreak havoc with their digestive systems, preventing food from passing. It could also be a tumor.

Exploratory surgery was in order, but that made everyone nervous. Macy was still critically underweight. Anesthesia carries a level of risk for any animal. In Macy's compromised health, that risk would be much higher. But if her digestive tract couldn't unblock itself, Macy's fate would be sealed anyway. Surgery it was.

Unfortunately, Animal Services had called when I was about to get on a flight. I would be out of reach until well after Macy's surgery. That meant a nerve-wracking six hours for me. By the time I was back on the ground, I was desperate for news. Happily, the news was good. As Macy was being prepped for surgery, the team had taken her for a walk in their enclosed courtyard, and she had a poop. The blockage seemed to have been either gas or leftover food. Surgery was averted, at least for now.

Macy's digestive tract wasn't done with us yet, however. A few days after Christmas, she passed a peach pit. There really had been a blockage, though it had been small enough that she could digest around it. She'd probably been scrounging in the garbage and come across a discarded piece of fruit. Anything is food when you're a starving dog. Macy was lucky, and lucky now to get rid of it (though it couldn't have been comfortable... ).

The good news continued. Macy would greet the New Year another three pounds heavier, topping the scales at 52 pounds! If she had an undetected health issue, there's no way she'd have been able to retain that kind of weight. Things were looking up for our girl.

~~~~~~~~~~~~~~

Macy's physical health was becoming less of a worry with each day. Staff had noticed another problem, though.

Macy was a dog, a beautiful dog. Everyone knew it, except her. She didn't seem to know what she was or how to behave. When the clinic staff had walked her in the exercise pad before her planned surgery, Macy had no idea what the leash was for or how to walk with a person. She was lunging all over the place. She still chomped and nipped at hands when offered treats. I've learned in rehabilitating dogs that there is a physical side to the effort that is easier to diagnose than the mental side. That's a journey that can take months, even years.

The staff worked with her as much as they could, but they were there to provide a safe haven and medical attention, not dog training. A slow-feeding bowl helped calm her eating, so she didn't scarf down her meals and give herself indigestion. We would also train her by putting her food bowl down and making her take a beat before eating. Learning that the food didn't disappear while she waited reduced her anxiety and gave her a sense of control. The round-the-clock care was improving her confidence, and that drove her recovery, but her social skills were nonexistent. That was going to be a problem when she was adopted, especially if there were other dogs in the home.

Some local dog-training experts reached out to us about helping. They worked with her on making eye contact, which focused her on the human offering her treats instead of the food in their hands. That would lead to less nipping of fingers. They worked her on rudimentary commands, like "stay" and "sit," and got her accustomed to walking on a leash.

By the middle of January, Macy's weight gain was slowing down. She was in range of what was healthy and normal for a dog of her size, and her appetite was steadying. She had gone past the month we'd originally planned for her to stay in Norco, but her recovery was at a stage where she could start meeting adoption applicants. And by staying at ACS, she could get spayed and maybe even get those teeth fixed.
~~~~~~~~~~~~~~

*Teaching Macy how to play with toys.*

We scheduled her first meet and greet with a family looking to adopt. We were considering local applications only so that if anything went wrong after the adoption I could go get her. I was committed to making sure she found the home she deserved. That was my promise in adopting her.

The first family showed up with their young kids and dogs. They'd followed Macy's progress online and were beaming with excitement to meet her. She didn't know what to make of the kids and mostly ignored them. That was fine. She didn't feel threatened by them, and that was the important thing. Then she met their dogs. The meet went downhill quickly. She didn't know how to interact with other dogs at all. She was slinking around the yard, then lunging into their space. That stressed the other dogs, and they started lashing out and trying to correct her.

Dogs have a natural behavior and expect other dogs to act the same way they do. When a dog's behavior is strange, it signals to other dogs that something's wrong. That's when you see the kind of response we were seeing from these two visiting dogs. It was clear that Macy wasn't ready.

We thanked the family for coming. I give them gold stars for being willing to try and adopt a special case dog like Macy, and I let them know they are superstars in my book. There's nothing wrong with admitting that a particular dog isn't a match. I never want people to adopt after a meeting goes poorly just because they feel sorry for a dog they see in a video. That just leads to dogs being returned to the shelter.

We tried a second meet and greet. The family had only one dog, and it was smaller than Macy. She snapped and barked a lot. We decided to pull her from adoption until we got her behavior under control. That's when yet another hero in Macy's story put on her cape. Miranda, who ran the daycare side of ACS, was also a dog trainer, and she offered to bring in her own dogs to help model and guide training for Macy. That's something Flip used to do for us, so I thought it was a great idea. The clinic supported it, too.

Macy was doing really well, and we tried another meet and greet. It was okay, but still not a match. I was getting worried. We'd been through all the viable local candidates.
I really didn't want her going across the country or up to Canada or

overseas (we'd received applications from as far as Germany). The chances an adoption could go off the rails were just too great with Macy.

Though the adoption process was stalled, Macy's health was stabilizing. She was finally ready to be spayed, and, more worrying for me, she could have her dental surgery. All those worn and broken teeth suggested she was going to need extensive repair, if her teeth were even salvageable.

A dog's ability to chew is so important for their physical well-being; it helps them get the nutrition they need, and it helps alleviate stress and boredom. Dogs love to wrestle the day away with frozen lick toys, safe chew bones, and other activities that use their mouth to engage and stimulate their brain. There's an aspect of mental exercise in chewing that Macy would sorely miss if all her teeth came out. From the first minutes I'd spent with her, I noticed how she scarfed her food and wondered if her teeth were giving her so much grief she couldn't chew without pain. I hoped the surgeon wouldn't pull too many. We even took her to a canine dental specialist renowned for their ability to provide titanium crowns and other teeth-saving techniques. It would be a big expenditure, but for a dog as young as Macy, giving her the best chance at having her teeth for the rest of her life was worth the money. Some people like fancy shoes, cars, or big diamonds—I just like my dogs whole.

We got lucky. She needed one tooth capped, and that was it! No extractions, no titanium crowns. Macy's teeth could recover along with the rest of her.

It was around this time that an early comment on Macy's first YouTube video resurfaced and caught our eye:

*The second she is allowed to be adopted, I can be there. I live in Arizona but am retired and have been waiting for the right dog. I'm a retired certified vet tech and can provide her with a big yard and all the love, time, and healthcare she needs. Please keep me in mind. I will be checking back with her story again...*

*Learning "recall" and "sit" with a trainer.*

Meeting her new mom. It was love at first sight!

Lots of people leave comments on videos saying they'd gladly take a dog. It's hard to tell if they're just saying it out of kindness or if they're really in a position to adopt. But in this case, the commenter had also filled out an application. I reached out to her, and she was only about four hours away. We had a few calls and lots of questions. I was nervous, but Sherri was making me optimistic. She and her husband had lost their beloved greyhound a few years back, and they finally felt ready to bring a new dog into their home. She had handled some difficult dogs and really understood a dog's need for human connection. She agreed to meet us halfway between LA and her home in Arizona.

Macy had put so much trust in me, and from the moment we'd bonded in that kennel, I'd promised her she would be safe. I was determined to see for myself that this was the right move before handing her over. I collected all the paperwork, got in the car with Macy, and hit the road. Macy was good company. She wasn't used to being in cars yet. She's a very affectionate dog as it is, but on that ride, she was extra cute!

We pulled up to the neighborhood ballpark where we were scheduled to meet. I was feeling good, and I turned around and said to Macy that I thought this could be it. This could be the path to your life being amazing. This could be how you get the life a dog deserves to live.

My intuitions were right on the money. Sherri showed up and it was love at first sight. Macy went right to her, wagging her tail, and Sherri crouched right down to meet her. Macy didn't stint on the nuzzles and dog kisses. I handed Sherri the leash. This was a home run.

Macy is a perfect example that we all need love just as much as food, water, or the air we breathe. Looking back, I've realized that any time in my life I've allowed myself to believe that I don't need anyone was likely when I needed people most. If we slow down and pay them the attention they deserve, dogs provide a constant reminder of this–and none more so than that emaciated German Shepherd who turned up starving in the middle of the night desperate for food, shelter, and medicine, but who was ultimately brought back to health and happiness by the deep bond she had the courage to form when I first met her.

Today, Macy is living happily ever after in Arizona. Sherri renamed her Lucy, which is close enough to Macy that she transitioned easily. The day she got to her new home, Macy...I mean, Lucy, ran around the backyard pool, exploring her new surroundings just like a regular dog. Every update we've got from Sherri since has been the same: The dog that had no cards left to play had gone all in on love–and won.

**_An emotional but happy kiss goodbye._**

# CHAPTER 5

# HONEY

# (A BAD REPUTATION)

SCAN TO LEARN MORE
ABOUT HONEY'S STORY

**Picture this: Someone says to you, "There's a really cute brown and white Goldendoodle puppy in that kennel right over there, named Ziggy. She has a pink collar on, and she is so happy and playful and fun. Go right in and meet her."**

Meeting Ziggy sounds pretty appealing, right? You would probably march right over to that kennel, open the door, and say, "Hello, Ziggy!" You'd be petting her, and you'd be so happy, and the dog would wag her tail and give you kisses.

Right?

Now, imagine that someone said that to you, but the dog was jet black and had been attacking other dogs. You see that she has pressed herself against the rear wall of the kennel and appears to be extremely anxious. Oh, and by the way, her name is Venom.

How excited are you to step into that kennel now?

---

I could tell from the moment I saw her that I was going to have to take it slow.

She was curled up in the back corner of one of the smallest kennels in the shelter. The sign on the door made it extra clear:

"HELLO! I'M NEW HERE! PLEASE *GO SLOW* WITH ME AS I ADJUST TO MY NEW ENVIRONMENT. THANK YOU!"

When I stepped inside and asked in as friendly a tone as I could muster, "Hi, can I come in and sit down with you?" she growled. I wasn't feeling threatened. She was a good-sized dog, but not intimidatingly large. An all-black shepherd mix, I guessed, though probably mixed over so many generations, you'd never figure out her lineage.

That's not too bad, I thought. She'd only growled once and hadn't moved. More of an "I'm unsure." Winning this girl's trust was going to be all about taking my time. I crouched down, leaving some space between her and me–as much as I could in a four-by-six kennel–so she could come to me when she felt ready. Curiosity can do a lot to temper fear. I broke off a piece of jerky stick and tossed it softly in front of her to see if she would take it.

Being an all-black dog and hiding at the back of the dimly lit kennel, this girl wasn't easily going to appeal to potential adopters. She still had that sign on the door, so I figured we had at least a week before she was through her ten-day freeze on adoptions. That should be long enough to warm her up and convince her to take an interest in people as they came past.

Hesitant but definitely interested, she took the treat. That was something we could work with. I sat down, feeling no sense that she was going to get aggressive, and put another treat down a little farther away from her, to see if she'd stretch her neck to get it. She did! So I tried handing her a piece in my fingertips. Nope.

I don't take it personally when a dog isn't willing to leave their comfort zone for one of my baked treats. This girl needed time. She was scared, and as far as I knew, she had no reason to trust a human locked with her inside a tiny cage. Maybe she even had reason to fear people.

That's when Alexis came along with the details. The dog's adoption hold wasn't just beginning; it was nearly done. She had been here just under ten days! That sign on the door suddenly wasn't just a note of caution, it was a declaration that this poor dog had been in this fear state for over a week.

This was not good.

---

If I tell you I have a friend who gets angry when people approach them, even if that friend is actually the friendliest person in the world, then you're going to approach them with trepidation. They're going to start wondering why people are behaving so strangely around them, and that could even lead to them getting—you guessed it—angry. Suddenly an inaccurate impression becomes a self-fulfilling prophecy.

If this shepherd mix was like this a week after arriving in the shelter, I could only imagine what kind of mood she was in when she first got there and the impression she'd made on the staff. She didn't seem prone to aggression, but something had made that sign on the door feel necessary.

I was determined to break down this dog's fear state and spark her curiosity in me. I wasn't sure how far we'd get, given her reluctance, but we had to open her up more than this. Given how long she'd been here, the stakes were high.

I offered her a whole jerky stick while looking away, to avoid intimidating her with eye contact. Between the other dogs and some loud vehicles passing on the road outside, the shelter was extra noisy that day. All the racket wasn't helping calm this dog's nerves. But a snack that large is tough to refuse, and she took it off the floor. I tried another piece, in my fingers, and she took it, too. This was good! I tried another, on the floor and far enough that she'd have to stretch out again. She just curled up.

We tried one of my new tricks, the Pac-Man treat trail. I broke off small pieces of jerky and made a line leading away from the dog, so as she took each one she'd have to extend herself farther and farther to reach the next one. The results were mixed. Still, I encouraged her, told her she was a good girl, and even started brushing her paw with my hand after handing her treats. Some dogs are affection driven; if I can get them to trust me enough to pet them, they just open right up in response to gentle touch.

She was definitely looking at me, daring herself to make a moment's eye contact. This was all good.

Once Alexis gave me the background on this dog, the huge disconnect I was seeing between her quiet demeanor and her bad reputation suddenly made a lot more sense.

"Her name is Venom."

I had to ask Alexis to confirm I'd heard correctly. I had.

***Trying to win her affection with my treats.***

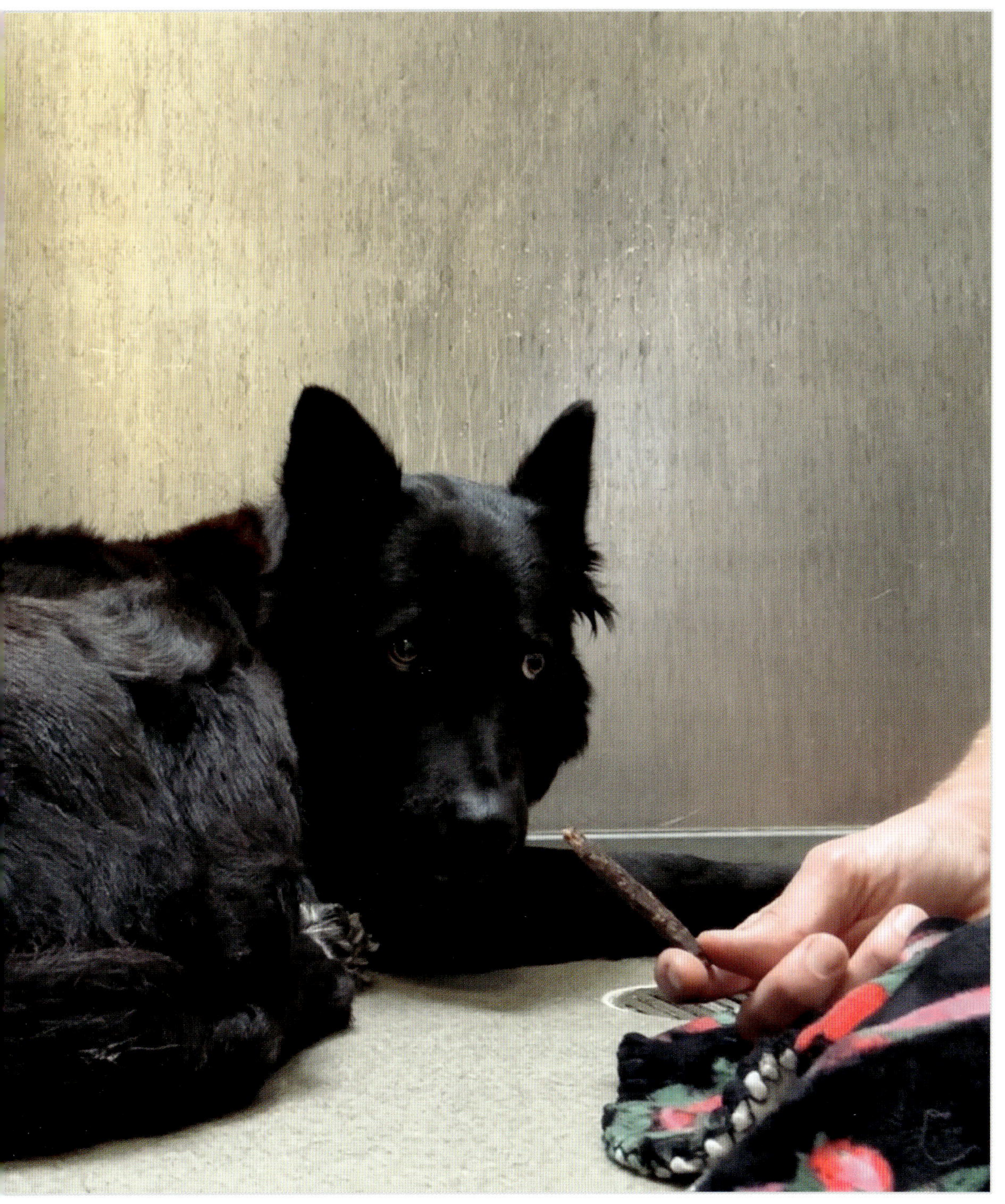

"This is her second time here," Alexis added. That drove it home. No wonder this dog was in such a state. I was reminded of big Casper, another dog so devastated to be back in the shelter he had frozen in place, on his feet, and refused to fall asleep.

The first time Venom (I couldn't believe anyone could call her that) was here, she had been found running around after the owners had gone on vacation, and they'd picked her up when they got home. This time, after someone had found her and brought her in, the owners didn't respond to the shelter's attempts to reach them for a week. When the owners finally responded, they said she had escaped the yard, but they didn't want her anyway; she hadn't been nice to their smaller dog.

And that was it for Venom.

Well, Venom's story needed to end right there. It was time for a new story, and that would be Honey's story.

When I was a kid, I used to wonder who named hurricanes. I was so curious about it, I wanted that to be my job when I grew up. I'm glad it's not, because now I'm in charge of naming dogs, which does a lot more to make them and their families happy than naming a hurricane has ever done for anyone.

A dog's name really matters. I can't stress this enough. I've named more dogs than I can count, and my only regret is that I don't have more time to think about what I call them. A bad name, like Venom, can taint that dog's interactions with people. If a dog is treated for long enough like it's something to be scared of, and not like a dog who could be friendly and loving, the dog's behavior could start to reflect that.

I come from a family that didn't have much. We survived on donations and vouchers and whatever we could get our hands on to make ends meet. That left me with a sense of insecurity because of all the things we didn't have. But one thing I did have, which was almost a superpower in guiding me toward the person I wanted to become, was my name.

I'm not native Hawaiian, but I was born there, and my mother was Henai. That's a traditional Hawaiian practice of welcoming someone into your family—not just making them feel like family, but making them family! It's not something we really have on the mainland, but it's a way

Assuring her we're going to get through this together.

of life amongst traditional Hawaiians. So when I say she was Henai, I mean she had been welcomed into a family, and by extension so was I. And to this day I am grateful for what that means to me.

When I was 1 month old, I was named in a ceremony by Auntie Nona Beamer, a Hawaiian elder and icon. She passed in 2008, but she had long been a champion of the traditional Hawaiian culture. She helped bring hula back into schools, as it had been banned by missionaries. I was so lucky to have my name dedicated to me by such an important figure.

My full name is He kanaka e hana ana no ke akua. Auntie Nona realized that my name was a bit long for everyday use, so she said, "We will just refer to him by 'Kanaka.'" ("Rocky" was given to me by my family.) My name in its entirety translates roughly into "The Good Man Who Well Serves the Lord." "Akua" means "The Lord," though not necessarily the religious figure of Western tradition. I take to heart the idea of service and helping others, and my way of serving has been helping animals with the problems we humans created for them. To be given this name is a great honor, and I live my life to do everything possible to carry the Aloha spirit to others.

I share all of this with you because I see many dogs in shelters who have never had a name. If nobody has ever cared enough about you to give you a name, you can just imagine how you were treated by your owners. Your name allows you to love, and it allows you to be loved. It always pains me to meet a dog with no name, or who's just called Dog.

So in the kennels, as I have taken on more responsibilities over the years, it's become my job to name dogs whose names are either unknown or really bad. Venom was one of the latter. I know it was probably inspired by Spiderman comics and movies, but when I meet a dog with a name that is aggressive–combined with a family that doesn't care enough to come pick her up–I can't help but fill in the gaps and make assumptions. That's a dog who needs someone in her corner standing up for her.

Even if we just give a dog a temporary nickname, something lovable and endearing, families can decide when they adopt whether to change it to something meaningful to them, like how Macy became

***Seeing hope in her eyes for the first time with her new name.***

Lucy. To name someone sincerely is an act of love, and even if a dog can't understand the meaning of the name, it can make a real difference in their quality of life.

~~~

The sweet black dog—I'm done calling her Venom—was sitting with her head up now, better than before, but still pointed behind me and not engaging directly. Her front paws were stretched out in front of her, not curled up. That was good.

I was suspicious of the whole story about her being mean to a smaller dog. Fear and anxiety can make a gentle dog act out of character, but usually when owners who care about a dog face any sort of behavioral problems they at least try to help. They go online and look for training videos, reach out to a local trainer, and shelters sometimes have resources to share. You could just call the shelter and be honest: "Hey, I'm considering turning my dog in because of such-and-such behavioral problem and we don't know what to do. Can you give us any guidance before we give up?" But when a family is happy to let a dog escape and avoids calls from the shelter (again)? I'm not so sure.

I wondered, if she'd had the name Venom for all of her life (she was three years old), how have people been treating her? And did anyone notice or care? I was getting the feeling that this dog hadn't stood a chance from day one. If we were going to turn her fortunes around, she needed a name that was the complete opposite of Venom.

I asked Alexis, Honeysuckle? Sugar? We kept it simple and sweet: Honey.

"I love you. You are a good dog," I told Honey. She turned her head from where she was lying on the floor beside me, and for a tiny moment, she made eye contact. It didn't last more than a second before she pointed her face back towards the rear of the kennel. It was just a moment, but it was a huge step. *Maybe*, she was realizing, *just maybe, this person isn't so bad*.

I always wonder what the real magic of positive affirmation is. Is it how my voice sounds as I'm saying good things about the dog, and saying them with conviction? Did Honey pick up on that tone? Did she know the phrase "good dog"? I hope she did (she does now...but more on that later). Or is the power of these affirmations all in the effect they have on me, just saying them? Does just saying these things out loud remind me to see the dog
~~~

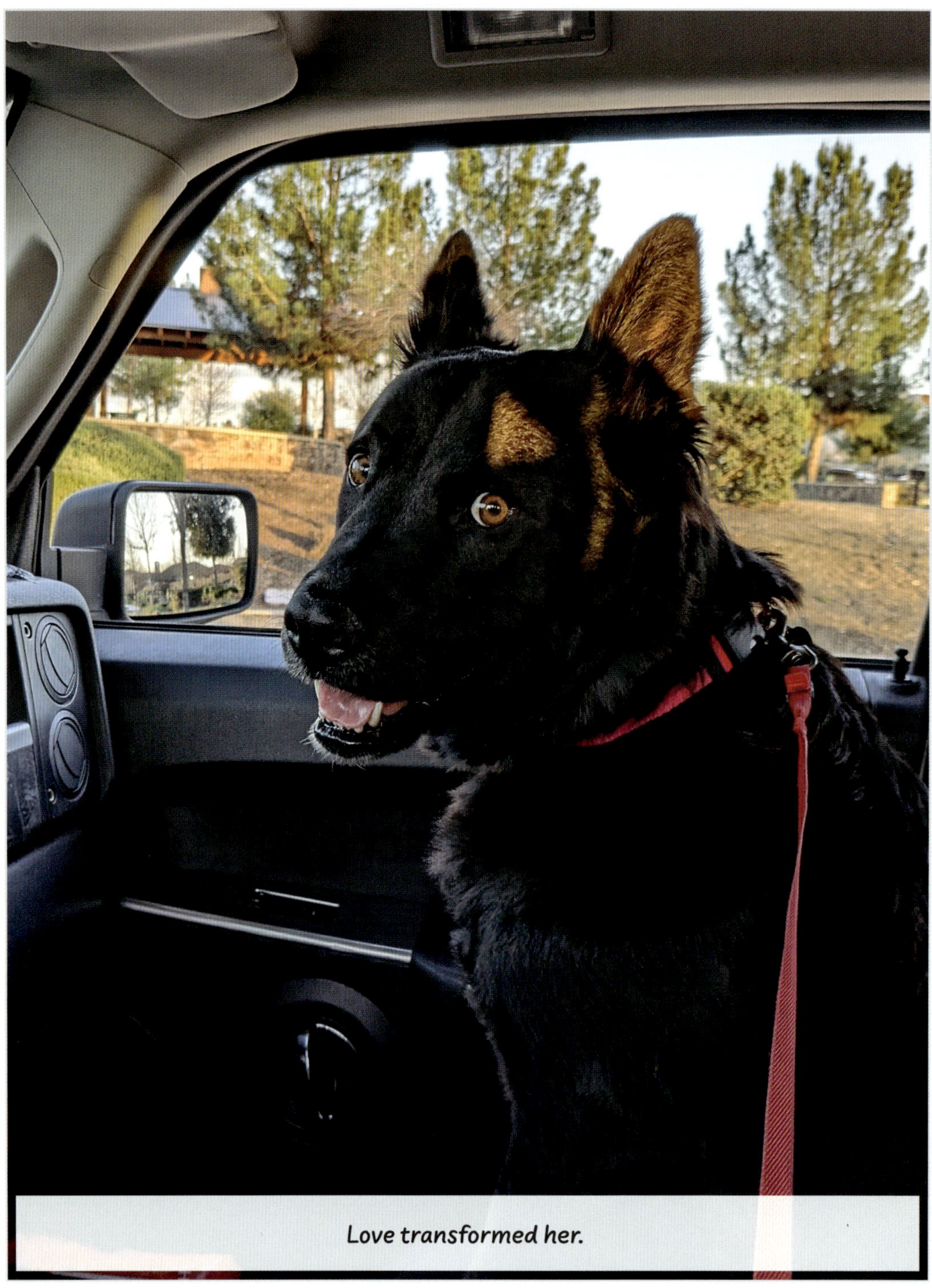

*Love transformed her.*

that could be instead of the sad, withdrawn animal I found when I arrived?

No matter the effect, when I gave her that name and spoke to her as Honey, I saw her in a different light, softer and sweeter. I could see the characteristics in her face and eyes. All I could think was that none of this was her fault: her being here for the second time, even if she really had been going after a smaller dog or jumping fences; and the ugly name that would make anybody think twice about greeting her in a friendly way. These things had defined her, and they didn't need to do so for one second more.

~~~

You might notice I always have a lead hung over my shoulder when I'm sitting with dogs. I don't use it very often, as I'm usually meeting shelter dogs in what is essentially a locked cage. But with Honey, I decided to put the lead to good use.

Honey was proving tough to warm up. I wanted to give her the scoop, but she really did seem too hesitant to accept more than the lightest of pets. I wondered if the pressure on her was getting too intense.

I took off that lead and dropped it gently over her head. She had a collar on (and had arrived with a collar of her own, though she didn't seem too crazy about it when I showed it to her). So it made sense that she didn't react poorly to me putting on the lead.

We walked around the kennel as much as the tiny space allowed, but it worked—a little. Prompted by the lead, she got up and moved around, as if to follow beside me. Like the eye contact, the "walk" didn't last long. But Honey was warming up; I could feel it.

When she settled onto my blanket, I tried petting her back leg as I gave her treats, hoping she'd associate contact with the snack. She stopped eating, so that didn't work. I turned my back and left the treat just sitting in view, pinched between my fingers. She was laser-focused on it, but left it alone. The treats were going to work; we just needed time.

Some dogs need a lot more time than others. They might have bruised spirits, like Honey, and when you bring them home, they might need a few days, weeks, or even months of hiding in a corner of the home or under the bed. You just make the space as comfortable as you can and let them decompress.
~~~

Honey out at a busy mall.

Time doesn't heal all wounds, but all wounds need time to heal.

"Honey, you are a good dog," I said. She yawned. Again, I didn't take it personally. It's hard for dogs to sleep in the noisy shelter, and even if they can handle the racket, some won't let their guard down long enough to get any rest. Honey's big yawn could have been her finally allowing herself to feel the fatigue that had built up after nearly ten days.

When I tried again with the treat, she let me pet her hind leg. Honey's demeanor was changing, even if she wasn't quick to trust. She was shifting her weight to be more face forward and was holding her head higher. She was facing the door like you'd expect a dog to do, her legs stretched out in front of her.

We spent a little more time in that kennel. She let me pet her head and softened up a little more. When I stopped, she looked at me and sniffed my hand. Yes! I rubbed her head some more and she seemed to melt.

I try to rub a dog's head right between the ears and give them that relaxed feeling that anyone who's gotten a good head rub knows. My hope is that it stays with

*Training to be a working dog.*

them long after I leave. And although this wasn't an issue with Honey, petting a longer-haired dog where the hair is shorter avoids tugs and painful pulls if their coat is matted.

I couldn't stay all day, as much as I wanted to. But when I returned to say hello to Honey about twenty minutes later, she wasn't hiding at the back of her kennel. She was standing at the door to greet me! True to form, it didn't last long. But that kind of progress gets dogs adopted into loving homes. And, I'm pleased to report, it worked for Honey.

What's in a name?

Enough that when a dog rescuer and shelter volunteer named Michelle saw Honey's transformation after we changed her name, Michelle saw something in this dog that she knew could continue to grow.

Michelle and her family adopted Honey, and Honey's transformation has indeed continued. Honey loves to go out in public, to the dog park, hiking trails, or the mall. She's "mild-mannered" and "sweet," Michelle told me, and is always game for adventures with her new family.

But Honey didn't stop at getting a new family. She got a new name. Not only is she treated like royalty, she is named like royalty: Empress Puppentine (Puppa for short). She also got a job!

Puppa made it through the selection process to become trained as a service dog and works with a family member with disabilities who has had a longtime need for exactly such a companion.

She is now living up to who she can be. We've gotten so many happy reports from Michelle, and she and her family just can't understand how anyone could cast an amazing dog like Puppa away or think she was anything but a beloved member of the family.

There has been no sign of Venom.

It was all in a name.

*Comfy in her new home.*

# CHAPTER 6

# VALERIE

# (OVER THE RAINBOW)

SCAN TO LEARN MORE
ABOUT VALERIE'S STORY

**About a year after Flip passed, out of nowhere my daughter told me she was very sad that Flip was gone and didn't understand why he couldn't just come back now. I didn't want her to be sad and remembered a story from the famous Vietnamese Buddhist monk Thich Nhat Hanh that I believe went something like this:**

*You look into the sky and see a cloud. There's my beloved cloud that I love so much. But the cloud goes away, it dissipates, as clouds do. You might say that the cloud has passed away. But later, as you sit and drink your water, you can look in the glass and see, hey, there's my cloud that I loved so much. It became water and the water became rain and now it's here, with me again. Just different.*

Our dogs pass on, eventually, but what I was trying to teach my daughter is that they're never really gone. I've been sad to see many dogs pass on. But these days, my cloud is Flip. At the time I'm writing this book, it's been just about a year since he died. His cancer returned. He was eleven, not a bad run for a boxer. But still, too soon.

I'm okay, but I miss him so much. With the time that's passed, I'm starting to process his passing in a new way. He's not there in the morning when I wake up or in the evening when I get home, but I do feel him with me, especially when I'm helping other dogs, something he was so good at.

It's just different now.

---

A red patterned blanket was hanging in the kennel window. The shelter didn't want the public to see inside. Maybe a mother was giving birth or maybe a dog was being sequestered because of a legal case. But experience taught me that there was probably a dog in that room whose condition was so bad they couldn't be even considered for adoption.

I steeled my heart before I stepped into the area where the public wasn't allowed and looked through the glass door of the kennel. She was curled up in a large, quiet room—much bigger than the tiny kennels I usually sit in. She was lying on a thick blanket and surrounded by stuffed animals. In the cozy space the staff had taken such care to prepare for her, the sight of the emaciated Pit Bull hit me hard. Incredibly, she would soon do everything in her very limited power to lift my spirits.

*After everything, she still has hope in her eyes.*

The pittie was grey and white, a mix of some sort, and seemed to be asleep. I didn't know if I should go in and sit with her. She had been fed and put through health-check, and now she needed to rest: Eat small meals, drink water, and sleep. I'd worked with enough dire cases that I knew the routine by now.

But as I crouched outside the glass door, her eyes opened and she, struggling but as quickly as she could manage, got up and walked forward to greet me! Unbelievably, even in her condition, this dog was friendly. That settled it. I was going in. I went to grab some treats first, and when I returned she was already curled up and resting on her blanket again. I backed in quietly, not wanting to startle her. She'd already convinced me that I could skip the crouch, and I sat down beside her.

Only a foot away now, I got a better look at her condition. She was a beautiful dog, or she should have been. Her spine and ribs were sticking right out. All her fat and muscle had wasted away. I could see the concave shape of her skull, which was almost the size of her torso. She was skin and bones, and she didn't even raise her head now; it was clearly such an effort.

The excitement I'd felt when she greeted me at the door passed. I took a very deep breath and my heart sank as the reality of her situation became clear. I didn't know her story, but she was either mistreated or very sick. And if it was neglect, it must have been going on for a long time for her to be this skinny. I also noticed her nails were really long. It's not likely that she was on the streets, because any dog on the streets around the area of this shelter would be noticed well before they could get this bad. But that meant somebody had allowed her to fall into this condition. No animal deserves this.

I needed to get out of my spiraling thoughts. This dog needed me to be present, not lost in my own sadness. So I reminded myself that her story didn't have to be a tragedy. This was going to be the turning point for her, the day when her life started to get better. And I thought about what "better" could look like six months from now.

She could be happy and full, and a healthy weight, sleeping on a comfy couch next to a warm fire on a cold January day. And she's just had her second breakfast because Mom didn't check with Dad before dishing it out to make sure he hadn't fed her already, which he had. And when

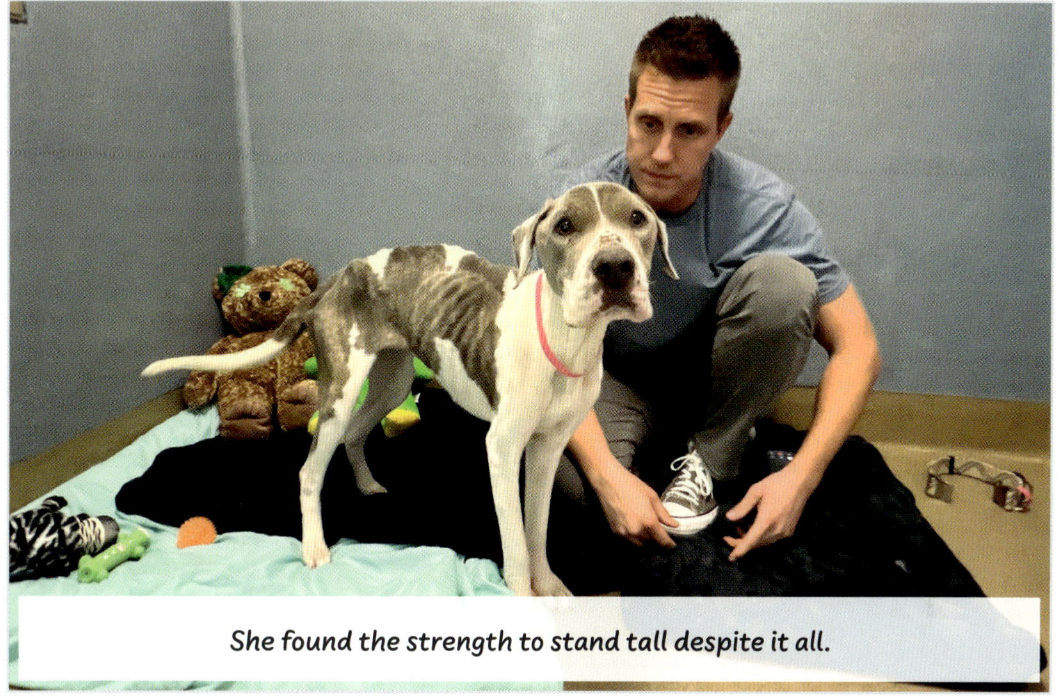

***She found the strength to stand tall despite it all.***

Mom asked if she'd eaten yet, of course she got excited and acted like she was hungry so she could get seconds. That sounded like a happy dog's life to me.

I broke off a piece of jerky stick and held it in front of her nose. To my amazement, she lifted her head and grabbed it! Of course she was hungry, but she was as comfortable about taking food as she had been about greeting me at the door. It's telling that with so little energy, the one thing she found the strength to do besides eat was try to make a new friend. I was falling in love with the spirit of this dog.

The spirit was willing, but the body had only so much to give. She ate the treat and curled up to rest.

Sitting with her, I thought about times in my life when I was pretty down and out. When I felt like that, I used to put my shoes beside the bed when I went to sleep at night so in the morning, if I could slip them on, lace them up, and keep moving, I'd know I could get through the day and move forward. I wanted to give the pittie something like that, though I was starting to think she already possessed the attitude to get through this, and it was me who had to pick himself up for the job.

As routine as it is, the health check hadn't detected any disease or major condition, nothing that would cause the dog to lose so much weight. Alexis caught me up on the pittie's story. She had been dropped off by someone who'd found her, and she didn't have a microchip. She wouldn't have had the strength to escape her owner, so she might have been dumped. The person who'd put her in night drop had left all their contact details, so it's a good bet they weren't the owner lying about their identity. Neglectful owners don't usually tell the shelter who they are.

Sometimes a dog found in this condition does lead to charges against a negligent owner. But resources for this are few, and they're better spent helping the dog recover and find a new home. Dogs are still legally considered property in the US, and it's up to those of us who care about them to advocate for stricter laws and prevent animal neglect. It's worth thinking about when you're deciding who to vote for in your local elections. We need people in charge who won't leave it to shelters and emergency animal-care workers to stop dogs from ending up like this one.

The pittie was certainly doing her part to put on weight. She devoured every treat I put in front of her nose. She took them from my fingertips, my open palm—she was not shy. I gave her larger pieces and some head rubs and scratches on the hindquarters. Her skin was quite scabby, so I had to watch where and how firmly I touched her.

She was all for the treats and love, and I figured she was becoming comfortable enough with me to consider the scoop. I moved closer to her and pulled her onto my lap. She just kind of flopped, with her head hanging over my thigh. Again, she seemed too weak to hold her head up. And again, when I put a treat in front of her, she found the energy! When she flopped again, I was feeling bad, but comforted that she was settling in with the warmth and contact that the scoop allows her to have.

Then I realized she was pulling a fast one on me. Her head was hanging over my leg as if she were exhausted (which she was). But she was also stretching to reach a whole treat stick that I'd left on the blanket. She got it too! I broke it in pieces for her—but finders keepers. I loved that even in her condition she wasn't above a little mischief.

One thing always strikes me when I'm holding a dog that's in such terrible condition, when they have given their all and just can't keep going. It's how heavy their head becomes. Often when I scoop a dog that is emaciated, sick, or has not slept for days, their neck muscles can barely lift their head. When I give it a little rub or support its weight for them, I can feel their neck muscles release in gratitude. It's as if, by holding their head I'm taking the weight of their world into my hands, even just for a little while. In these moments, I am so grateful that I am there in that exact moment to be the support they have so long deserved.

She had a collar with her. It was surprisingly new looking, which I took as another sign that she hadn't spent long on the street. She sniffed it when I held it close but she didn't react at all. It didn't seem to spark any memories of happy walks—or the opposite. Out of curiosity, I put the collar over her head. There was a huge gap between her neck and the collar. I could have put my hand through it, her neck was now so much smaller than it used to be.

The collar didn't have any information on it, and with no microchip she was nameless. We needed to call her something—and something

**Helping her hold up her head.**

good. I kept the head rubs coming. It was really surprising to me that this animal was so trusting and so eager for human company. Dogs never cease to amaze me.

Eventually, she really did start to snooze on my lap, with her head resting on my arm. Emaciated as she was, she was still a big animal. I'm so grateful to be large enough to handle a large dog like this. These moments are awesome. I was content just spending this time with her.

~~~

Alexis and Kelly thought of calling her Valerie. I liked the name immediately, and even more after Alexis told me why they suggested it. It means healthy and strong, which we all wanted her to be, and which she was in spirit. I couldn't have agreed more. We would call her Valerie.

I thought how much I'd like to take her to the farm, but it wasn't quite ready. She needed a committed rescue that was able to handle her intensive care from day one. Valerie would need more attention in the coming weeks and months than a shelter is equipped to provide. Although sitting amongst all these stuffed animals, I had to appreciate how much love they'd already put into her care.

I spent an hour with Valerie. It was hard to see a dog in that state, but so rewarding to give her the time. She made the most of it. I hoped those cuddles would help keep her spirits up for the long journey ahead. She took another whole jerky stick before I went, and her tail was wagging! Even in that condition, she could express happiness.

As I was leaving, she came to the door to see me off. We put out a call to rescues. Whoever had the honor of helping this dog would get back all the love they put into her recovery, and then some.

Valerie's amazing spirit inspired quick action from Lovebugs Rescue. In fact, Valerie was taken on personally by a member of the Lovebugs team, Kelly Hammons, and her husband so she could recover with them at home. Valerie didn't have much strength to walk, so they would take her for walks in a wagon. They put her in sweaters or pajamas and wrapped her in blankets, since she couldn't maintain her body temperature until she put on weight. They kept the jerky sticks coming too—now confirmed to be her favorite treat. They even kept her crated near the fireplace, just as I imagined might happen six months in the future, except it was happening for her right now.
~~~

**Being present in her lowest moments.**

It seemed like a dream come true for Valerie. But an ending that happy was a lot to ask of a dog who has been through so much. If you've been wondering why I'm telling Valerie's story alongside the news that we lost Flip, guard your heart. Because as we saw in Macy's story, there are so many ways that a dog so badly emaciated can fail to recover. Their kidneys might shut down. Their liver might stop working. Their heart might have been through so much stress that it just can't take any more. No matter how much you feed them, or how much love you show them, if the body can't recover all the necessary functions for life, we lose them.

*We lost Valerie.*

On her last day, Valerie woke up with Kelly, and her gums were pale and she wasn't moving. Kelly got her quickly to a vet, and X-rays showed that Valerie really did have a tumor. It was either on her liver or spleen and had ruptured. She was bleeding internally. The vet couldn't operate on her, as she was still too thin, and her blood pressure was dropping fast. A blood transfusion might keep Valerie alive a little longer, the vet told Kelly, but it wouldn't change the outcome. It was time.

Kelly and the rescue team struggled with the decision. Giving up wasn't in

**Getting to go on "walks" in her wagon.**

their nature. But she had watched as Valerie failed to put on weight, despite the care she was getting. And now it was confirmed she had cancer. There was nothing they could do that wouldn't just prolong Valerie's suffering. Valerie was going into shock. Kelly held her close until the end.

"If love could have saved her," Kelly said to us, "she would still be here."

---

Was Valerie a victim of neglect? Her loving spirit was so different from many dogs we see who have been through terrible mistreatment. Or had the tumor caused the weight loss and left her owner unable to cope and afraid they would have to pay for care they could never afford? We would never know.

What we did know was that we had been blessed to know this girl, even just briefly.

I struggled to get anything done on the day I heard the news. I was heartbroken. I spent some time thinking about the short time we'd spent with her, and in the end, I'll tell you I couldn't be more grateful that I was there with her in her final days—that so many of us were there for her. She knew the love of her foster family, and she left this world knowing she was loved, what real warmth is, and what a full belly feels like. That was a gift–to her and to us.

I have a drawer at home where I tuck away the kennel cards of dogs we've lost. These are the information sheets with everything the shelter knows about each dog. There's always a photo on them. I don't take them out very often. It hurts too much. But once in a while, I will look at them to remind myself just how important it is that we come together to tell these animals' stories and celebrate their spirits, and that we do it for the animals who really need us. When I look through those cards, those dogs are not nameless and they're not faceless. They've still got at least me loving them. And you, if you're reading this. And that keeps me going.

If you've ever loved a dog and lost a dog, you know how much it hurts. Maybe you've looked around and wondered: Why does nobody understand? Nobody is hurting as much as I am about this–why? Why does this hurt even more than losing a person? Why am I left feeling like I'm strange to experience this, like no one gets what I'm going through? And maybe it makes you angry.

Know that I get it. I see you; I feel you; I hear you. And though I can't know your exact pain, I know *the* pain. And that thing that's making you feel like you're strange? It might be that your heart is bigger than most. And the reason you feel your dog's passing more intensely than some people's is that your dog gave you so much love. Tell me what's so strange about mourning the loss of someone who was there every time you opened the front door, wagging their tail, ready to give you everything and anything unconditionally–no matter what you've done or said, what treat you haven't given them, no matter how ugly you acted.

Dogs love you. Always and forever. What I think is strange are people who don't miss a beat from a dog passing. Losing the amount of love a pet can give you every day can be debilitating. So just know that when you're heartbroken for a dog who has passed, it's normal. It's okay.

Even a year after Flip passed, some days it hurts so bad I don't know what to do. I would trade everything to have him with me again–the farm,

*Sitting with Dogs*, all the time I've spent with dogs, anything, just to feel normal. Maybe one day I'll have a dog who's close to what Flip was to me, but I'll never have another Flip.

I will tell you this. At the very end, when a vet service came to the house, I held Flip's paw in my hand and promised him that I would do more. I felt guilty that I hadn't done as much for him as I could have. I hadn't given him as much love in return as he'd given me. In those last few years, especially. We'd had kids and my attention was divided between them and Kobe and Zoey and all the other foster dogs we'd brought home.

That guilt is probably misplaced. I know that, but I don't feel it. Flip had less of me, so he just gave more to the kids. That was how good a dog he was. If I wasn't always there to reciprocate his love, he wouldn't act up, he'd share that love with other members of the family. Our firstborn, Capri, who got to spend a few more years with him, called him "Bip" when she was a toddler. He helped with the foster dogs too. He was always so good with the other dogs.

It's funny to think that we struggled so much to find a name for the farm or the coffee we grow on its land. We hadn't thought one up yet by the time Flip passed. I'm an entrepreneur, and I enjoy marketing and coming up with catchy names for the things we do, but for some reason I was stumped.

I was thinking about the farm and how we'd bought it in the first place so Flip could have a farm, a place to run. Kobe, too. A place where a blind dog could run around safely in the open air, a place where our kids could know that life, as well. I may have grown up poor, but living in a farm community did us good. As I puzzled over a name, it was suddenly like he was there with me, and I just knew. I went to Kelly and I said, "It's Flip! It's Flip Farms. Flip Coffee." How had I not thought of this already? "This is it, right?"

"Oh, yeah!" she said. "That's it!"

It's weird for me to think that all this came together at the end of Flip's life, because he and I had accomplished so much together, fostered so many dogs together. It feels like a starting line, not the end. It's as if Flip is saying to me, "I got you this far, now it's time for you to run the race."

Just know, if you're mourning the loss of a pet, or even if you're fearful that you might face such a loss in the near future, they're not gone. Like the cloud that's turned to rain,

*Soaking in the sunshine with Flip in his final days.*

they're with you still, and the love they shared will fuel you to do more, to help more, to make sure you pay attention to what you can bring to this life and those who share it.

I like to ask people a question about their dog, whether still alive or a dog who's passed. If your dog could understand you for a moment, I mean 100 percent truly comprehend the words you spoke, what would you say to them? And in turn, what would they say to you?

I know what I would say. "Flip, thank you for being there for me. I'm sorry for any moment when I wasn't ideal. Thank you for being the dog most people only dream of. Loving and patient, you were perfect. Even in the times when I got after you, it was never serious. I don't even know why I did. I should have just laughed it off and let you do whatever you wanted. I love you, and I'm sorry I didn't give you even more, that we didn't have more sits or naps on the couch, or chase more tennis balls together. I thank you for the inspiration that you've given me. I can feel you even when you're not here."

I think Flip would say: "What are you talking about? You were great, you were perfect. There wasn't one time you messed up, Dad. I love you. I'm proud of you. Thanks for being my best friend and my dad." I believe he would say all that, not because I was perfect, but because his love for us was.

I know one more thing he'd say: "Is there any way you can get me a fully loaded burrito from Chipotle and sneak it over here?"

Flip used to grab my food off the counter when I wasn't paying attention. He once ate a fully loaded burrito. The good news: There were no onions in it. (Onions are toxic for dogs.) The bad news? Boxers' digestive systems don't like strange food. The next day was rough!

Our dogs can't last forever, but we can give them the love they can carry over to the next life, over the rainbow bridge.

Kids know how love works. Sometimes when we're on the farm and it's been raining, or if we're in the car, our daughter looks to the sky and sees a rainbow.

"Hey, Flip!" she says. "Hey, Zoey."

And I smile.

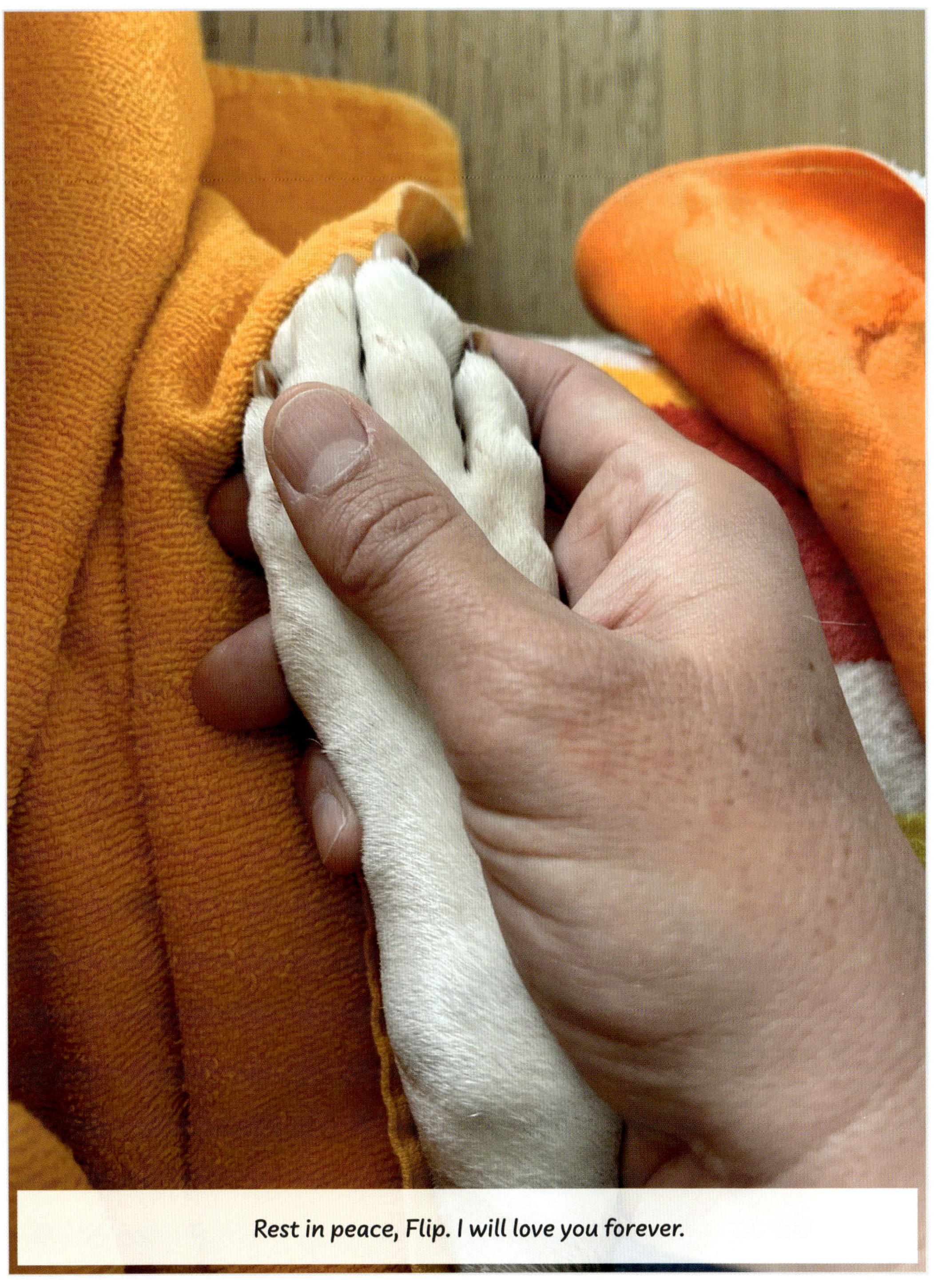

*Rest in peace, Flip. I will love you forever.*

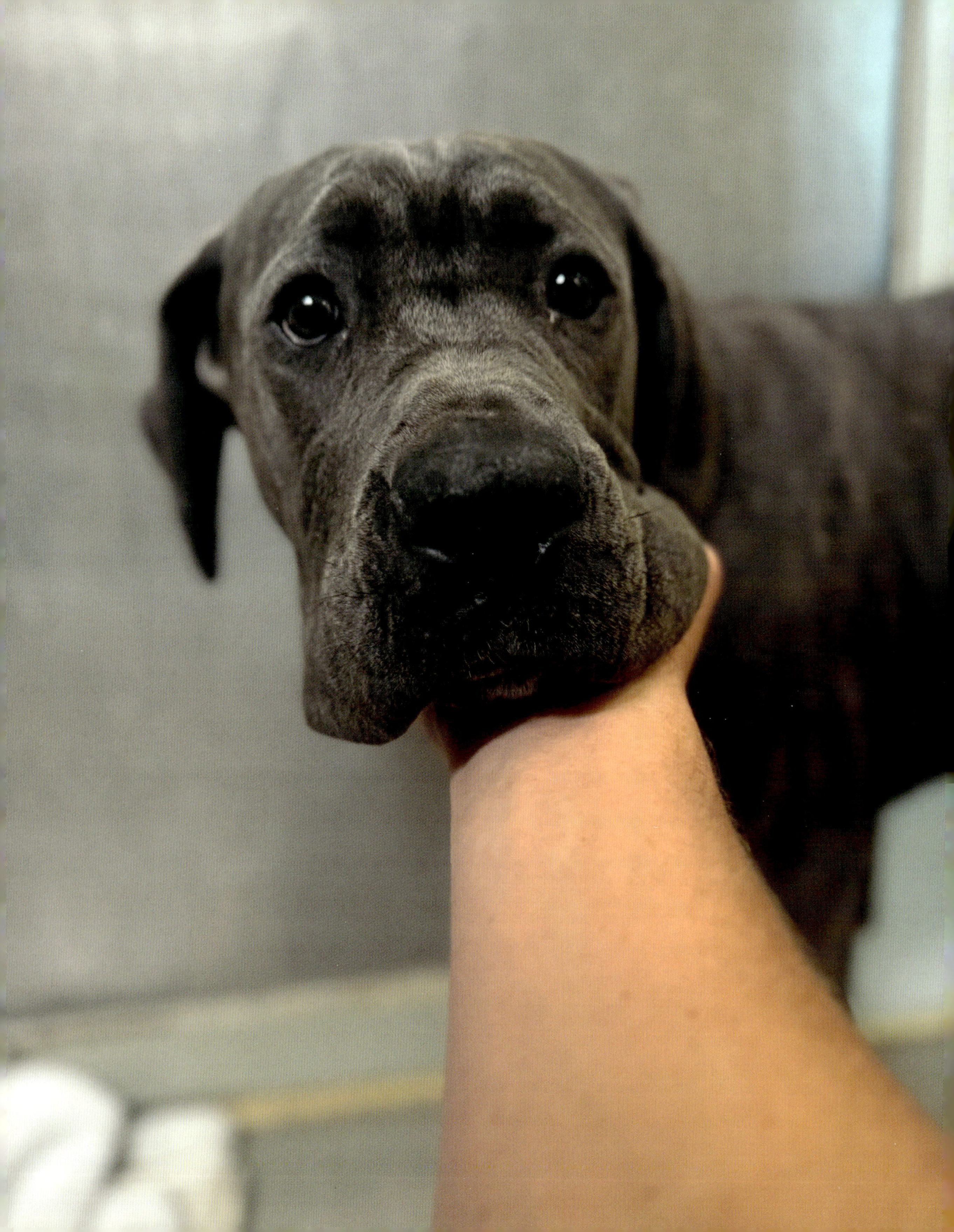

# CHAPTER 7

# MOOSE

# (THE GOOD BOY)

SCAN TO LEARN MORE
ABOUT MOOSE'S STORY

**I almost missed it.**

He was a younger dog, lying on the floor towards the front of his kennel, facing the hallway. He was large, some breed of Mastiff, grey brindle with a big white patch on his neck and chest. He still had those big, dark puppy eyes. The fact he was so cute and face-forward like that initially led me to pass him by. He seemed to be fine. As I was looking at the next dog, who seemed happy enough, I realized something about the young Mastiff that was so subtle I'd barely registered it. I thought, "Wait a minute," stepped back, and took a second look.

His foreleg gave a little twitch. I kept watching. Another little tremor, an uncontrollable shiver. He wasn't lying in the middle of the kennel because he was confident or dominant or any of the things we assume when we see a big dog. As I looked at him, his rigid posture and constant shaking were telling me a different story. This was a giant puppy in a state of trauma.

I didn't yet know what his story was, but a dog in fear will usually either glue itself to the back of the kennel, try to hide in a corner, or it might bark or–and this is rare and usually avoidable: charge the door. That's fight or flight–the common reaction to fear. But this dog's brain was telling him he'd lost all control of the situation–and it was definitely a bad situation. With no idea what to do, his body just shut down, frozen and helplessly waiting for whatever happens next. If anyone–you or a dog–spends too long in this state, it can do damage, mentally and physically. And there's often only one way out: the help of others.

Trauma stays with you in ways you don't expect. For years after my stroke, I woke up in the middle of the night with sweats, talking, or yelling. I would dream of being stuck in the stroke state, unable to communicate what was happening (shout-out to my old buddy Flip for that save). I learned that many stroke victims die at night because nobody knows they've had a stroke in their sleep, and even if they wake up, they are helpless to communicate what's happening to them.

Those nightmares ended recently, and I credit the dogs, our fans, and the work we do with shelter animals. Being open about life and sharing our vulnerability makes a difference. And every time I enter a kennel with a dog that doesn't know me, I make myself extremely vulnerable. It's not exactly like falling back into that stroke state, where you feel trapped underwater, but I do step into a tiny space that would be very hard to escape if the encounter with a larger dog went poorly. Every time I emerge safely, feeling deeply rewarded to see a dog better than I found them, a little piece of that trauma heals.

I'm no expert in trauma, but I've spent enough time dealing with it to know that we can pass through potentially traumatic events without actually being traumatized. I've heard the example of a kid being bitten by a dog, not breaking the skin or causing any damage, but still painful and frightening. That can be a traumatic event that leads to a lifelong fear of dogs. But if a parent, say, scoops you up right away after it happens, tells you it's okay, has you sit with the dog, and takes the opportunity to show you that you can't just take a treat away from it (if it was something so easily preventable that led to the bite), the whole biting episode might not leave such an impression. You might avoid the trauma.

That led me to the question I was facing as I stepped gingerly around the young Mastiff and settled in at the back of his kennel. Could I spend a few minutes with this dog that might prevent whatever horrible thing it went through from impacting the rest of his life?

I sat down on the kennel floor earlier in my visit with this Mastiff than I usually would. I couldn't sense any aggression in him, and I thought it would help to get as low to the floor as I could, making myself as small as possible. I spent a few minutes talking to the camera about all these thoughts on trauma, hoping the sound of my voice would comfort him enough to reduce any extra anxiety my presence was causing. I turned my back, in case he looked my way.

"We need to try some treats," I said, still talking to no one in particular.

He looked right at me! He knew that word, that was for sure. It was perfect: My back had been turned, so he didn't glance right into intimidating eye contact. I was a couple of feet away, just doing my thing and making him curious. When I said "treats" again out loud, he perked up. It was time to make good on the jerky sticks.

I broke off a small piece and put it near him. He went for it, but accidentally knocked it across the floor, too far away for him to be comfortable stretching out to reach it. Now I was facing a dilemma. Dogs in shelters have nothing to call their own. If he was food reactive and that treat was the only thing he felt belonged to him in his whole little world right now, he could become very upset if I reached for it. He might think I was trying to take his treat away. And if I moved too quickly, I could trigger a defensive reaction. And if I gave him a fresh piece, would I just compound his stress? These were all serious considerations, but I was overthinking it. The dog wanted a treat. I needed to keep it simple.

I moved slowly, kept my hand right against the floor in plain view, and pushed the piece of jerky closer to him. It worked! He gobbled it up. This was progress. He took another treat. I held one out to him in my fingertips. He drew the line at that. His nose was going, but he wasn't going to make eye contact or risk my hand being that close to him.

Still, this was good. By taking those treats and glancing in my direction when he hoped for another one, not only did he start seeing me as a friend, but I had brought him a gift. That gets other things working in his brain. The freeze starts to give way to his sense of smell, a dog's

***A giant puppy, he stopped me in my tracks.***

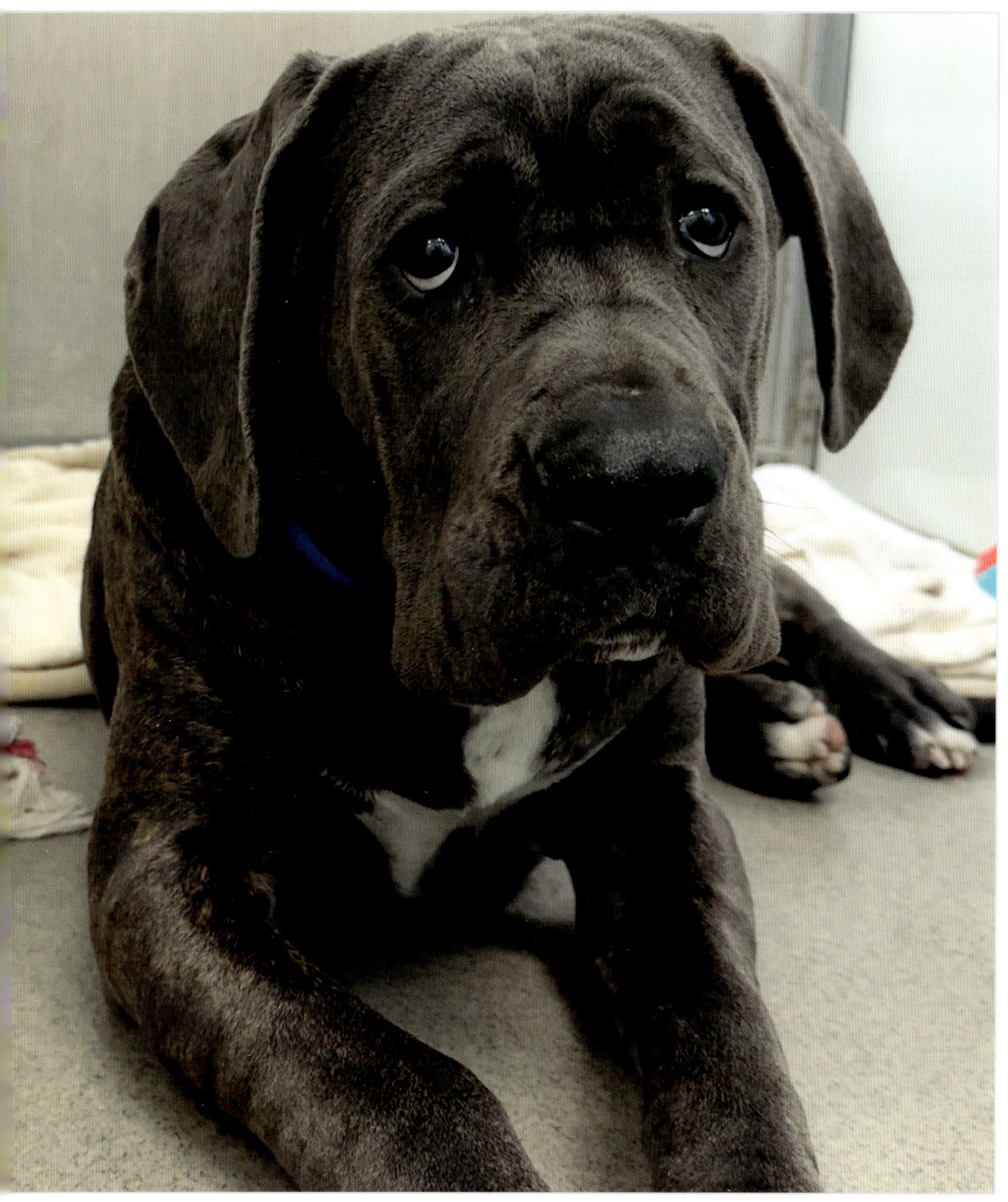

strongest sense, as well as taste. If we could start to release his brain from the fear state, then maybe we could make the trauma more manageable for him.

~~~~~~~~~~~~~~~~

It hit me as I sat there just how much he reminded me of a young Kobe.

I sneaked a few peeks, still trying to avoid eye contact. His eyebrows were incredibly expressive. I could tell what was going on inside there just from the look on his face. He was a gorgeous dog, muscly and thick-limbed with trimmed nails. He seemed to be in good condition. But he wasn't neutered, which he should have been by his age. Either someone hadn't taken the time to do it, or he might have been used as a stud dog. He's young for that kind of stress, especially around older female dogs who might not accept him without getting rough. Most breeders who are in business strictly for the money treat dogs poorly. This guy was a bit of a riddle.

Kelly had managed to get his story, but before we could get to that I noticed something in the tray on top of the kennel. It looked like a harness of some sort. The shelter holds on to collars and harnesses

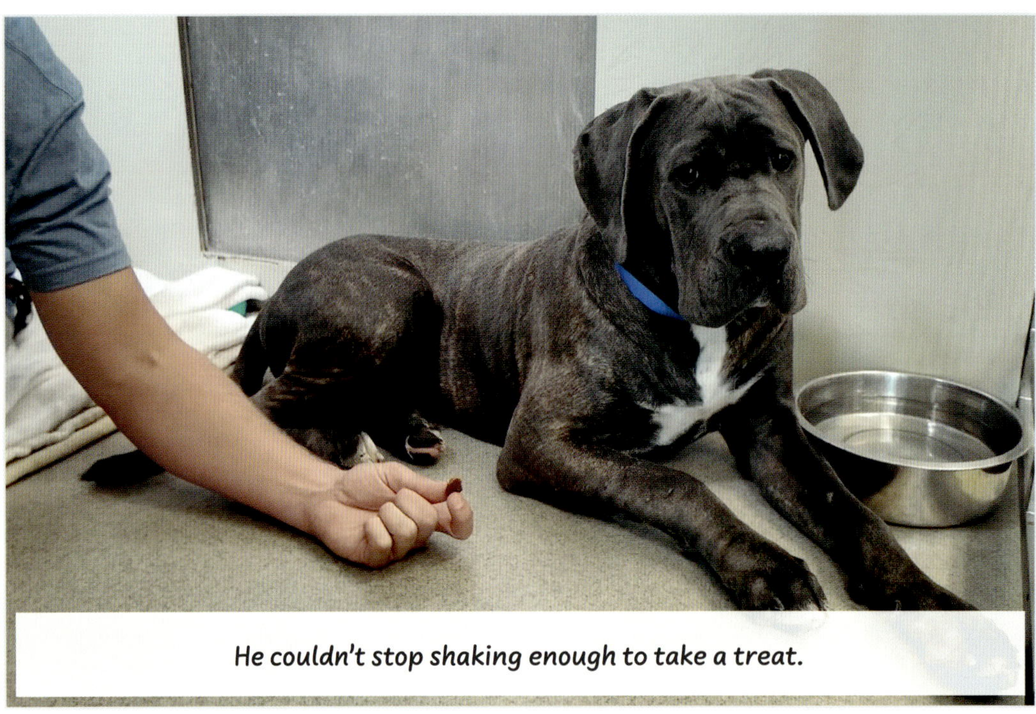

**He couldn't stop shaking enough to take a treat.**
~~~~~~~~~~~~~~~~

that dogs have on when they arrive. One, it belongs to the owner, who might turn up and be annoyed if the shelter threw it out. Two, it can help identify a dog to an owner looking for it, in the case that there are multiple dogs of the same breed and color in the shelter at the same time.

I pulled a pale pink lead out of the tray. It was a little unusual to see a pink lead for a male dog, but that didn't really mean anything. Strangely, the lead had a dirty white rope tied to the end of it. It went on and on, like a frayed piece of old fabric a clown would pull out of a hat. When I finally got to the end, it was in knots, making me wonder if it had been just tied around him as an improvised harness. That would not have been comfortable.

Sometimes when I present a dog's lead or collar, it gets a good response. It reminds them of going for a walk or spending time with their owners. But I have to be careful, because the associations aren't always happy ones. I showed the Mastiff, and he just curled back up in a ball. Maybe it wasn't his, or maybe it wasn't good. Either way, it didn't help.

I hadn't run into this since I started *Sitting with Dogs*.

Kelly had some background on this big sweetheart. It wasn't the Mastiff's first time at the shelter. That could explain his behavior, to an extent. He didn't want to be back here. It's not a comfortable place. It was probably traumatic for him the first time, and now he's going through it all over again. Plus, he was still very young. Being returned so soon after he'd been adopted was ringing alarm bells for me.

His first time in the shelter had been at six months. Someone found him running around in busy traffic. Animal Control brought him in. He was back now because apparently something bad had happened with the family cat, and the cat didn't survive. You can imagine, but you really don't need to. The facts tell you enough. It would have been traumatic for everyone.

I try to empathize when I learn a dog has done something that led to them being here. I want to give them positive affirmations, and I try to think about what happened from the family's perspective. Maybe this dog's family had rescued him with the best of intentions, but then he got ahold of their cat, for whatever reason, and that cat could have

He was trying to ignore me, hoping I would go away.

been a much-loved member of their family for years and years. Maybe they were stricken with grief and didn't know what else to do—or maybe they have other cats, and they couldn't keep him around for fear they'd be in danger.

We almost never learn all the circumstances that led to a dog entering the shelter, but sitting with that terrified Mastiff, I did know that what happened was an unfortunate event that really wasn't his fault. We breed these animals and raise them in spaces that, let's face it, are built for us, not them. They rely on us for guidance and protection and to teach them what we want from them. And though I had only limited knowledge of where this dog had come from, I knew that at least one promise to protect him hadn't been kept.

When he was adopted, his new owners would have had to sign an agreement in which they committed to neuter him. But they didn't get him neutered, so that tells me that there is more to his story. It could be they were overwhelmed and busy and were having trouble managing everything going on in their life. Was this the reason things got out of hand? It could mean they just didn't care, or maybe that they didn't have the funds. The failure to neuter and the tragedy with the cat were potential signs that maybe his owners were not 100 percent committed in the first place, especially for a dog this size.

If you really love your dog, you're their biggest advocate. Our dogs need that from us. Think of our Kobe, who's blind and has a glitchy heart. He gets over excited, can't see who's in front of him, and a few times he has barreled right over one of our little kids (and Kelly, more than once). There are tears, and he gets upset too, because he doesn't want to hurt his family. If you have small children and a big dog, you've probably experienced an accident like this–even if it's just a wagging tail knocking a child off balance or leaning affectionately against someone who has two little legs instead of four big ones. Nobody's happy when there's an accident, but it's on us to make sure boundaries are set to protect everyone, including our dogs, from the hurt feelings or worse that can result from preventable mishaps.

Kobe has a space that we section off in the house. He can't just go wherever he wants at any time of day. When he's with the kids for playtime, he knows it. When Kelly and I are getting ready early in the morning, he gets to hang out with us in our space and with the kids when they join us. In those moments, we can keep a careful eye on everyone. But when we aren't able to do that, Kobe goes into his space.

It's not his fault that he's a blind dog running over a little kid. We don't overreact, we prevent. That's our responsibility. Part of that prevention with Kobe is that we don't have a cat. We want one! But they are stealthy and quick, especially when they play. Learning how to handle a completely different kind of animal in his living space would stress him out and put immense pressure on his heart. Kobe's high anxiety and heart issues are always top of mind, and it's our responsibility to provide a calm, relaxing environment where he's able to thrive. It's why we don't take him out in public if it's not necessary–he's a great dog but the stress of meeting another dog is just not worth it.

You might have a reactive dog, one who lunges, barks, or growls when approached by a stranger or strange dog. If that's the case, you as the owner have a responsibility to say to someone approaching you and your dog, "Please stop. My dog is reactive and needs some space." Maybe they get offended, but advocating for your dog like that has to happen. It's a much better result than someone getting bitten. Or losing your cat. And maybe your dog, too.

Because of all the things in the world that can hurt our dogs, none of them can hurt them as profoundly as we can.

~~~

"You're a good boy," I said to the Mastiff in a higher tone of voice. I could feel the heaviness in my heart lift as I watched his face turn to me. In that moment, I could see what a puppy he still was, even at his massive size. He was sniffing the air and looking in my eyes. "I know you didn't mean it, and I know your family probably loved you a lot and that really bad situation happened."

He definitely responded to "good boy." Combined with some treats (he'd been gobbling up a Pac-Man trail, expanding his comfort zone), I thought we might be getting to the point where I could pet him. I tried. He started shaking again.

Kelly shared something else she'd learned from the shelter notes on him: "Scared of men, yelling and loud noises, and vacuums." Well, nobody likes the sound of a vacuum. Reacting to loud noise is typical for a Mastiff. But being afraid of men–that's a detail I don't always take at face value. There's no doubt this dog was afraid of me, and I'd been trying my best to be as unthreatening as possible. But my guess was it was something more than just an all-encompassing fear of me.

From what the staff had been told by the family members who'd surrendered the dog, after the incident with the cat, the male in the family had come down ferociously on him. Maybe it was raw emotional anger, maybe he thought he was teaching the dog a lesson. He was probably devastated, as well, at the loss of another family pet, a cat he might have been strongly attached to since long before the Mastiff joined their household. But using force to discipline this dog–with anger quite possibly getting the better of the owner's judgment–does no good, ever. And the terrible state the dog was in bore witness to that.

When dogs react with fear around men, I don't think the problem is that they're men, but instead that men often pick up this idea that they have to put up a front of strength and dominance when they're meeting dogs, especially shelter dogs. They've been told they need to lead the dog in an
~~~

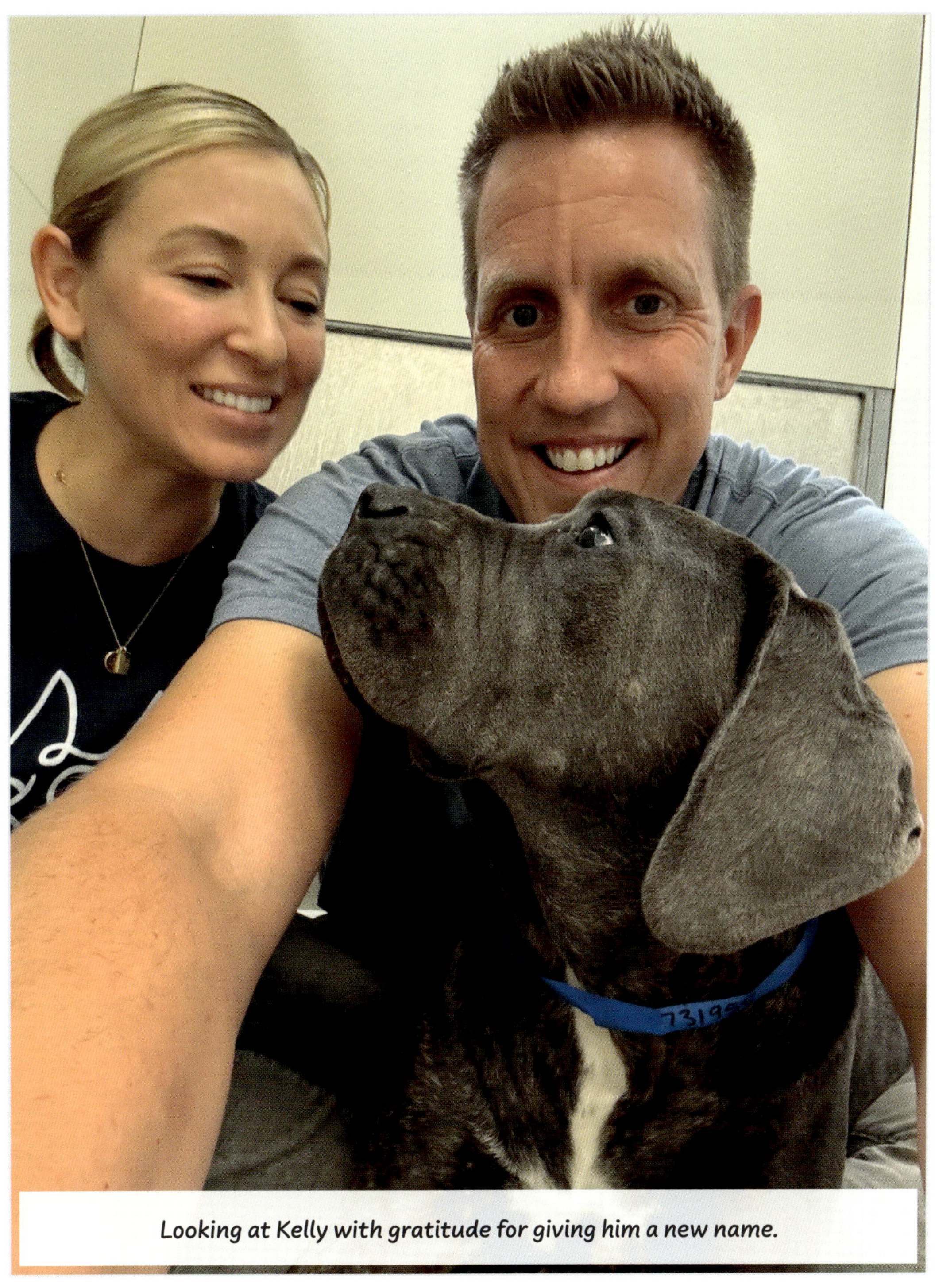

*Looking at Kelly with gratitude for giving him a new name.*

alpha-dog way. It's not how dogs work, especially not in shelters. We need more men working and volunteering in shelters (if only because we need more people helping out in shelters), but we need to meet these animals with vulnerability and our hearts on our sleeves. Nobody will see through your tough-guy front more quickly than a dog. If you meet them with kindness and vulnerability, there's nothing to see through. It's real—you're real—and it's what they need from you in the moment. You might even find that when you open your heart this way you are stronger than you ever thought possible.

Kelly told me the Mastiff's name was RIP. We didn't know if it was supposed to be said like a word (she had a childhood dog named Rippy) or said as the initials (R-I-P). Either way, I didn't like it—I mean, I hated it. I've told you how much stock I put in the effect of a dog's name. With the whole cat situation and now him being in a shelter, a name that was too close to Rest in Peace (R.I.P.) sent shivers through my spine. I put it on my list of things to deal with. The name RIP was going to be put to rest.

~~~

The Mastiff started taking treats from my fingertips. This was good. He had been a tough nut to crack, but I seemed to be getting somewhere with him. I tried some pets on his hindquarters and then the top of his head. He allowed me to scratch him between the eyes (Kobe's favorite), but his hind leg was shaking like a leaf the whole time. We weren't there yet.

I wanted to think up a new name but thought I'd try to put him on the lead in the meantime. He wasn't going to unwind just sitting there thinking about how scared he was. I dropped it carefully over his head and kept it loose. If he'd had a rough time on the leash at home and wanted to get out of it here, I didn't want him thrashing in this tiny space to get free.

"You want to go for a walk?" I asked him, keeping a high tone in my voice. He stood right up. I led him around the kennel a bit; we could only go a couple of steps in any direction. And of course, he went right for the front door. Why wouldn't he? He wanted out of this place! But I wanted him away from the front of the kennel, where he had plastered himself to the floor. I had the scoop in mind, so I sat myself down with my back against the side wall. I kept scratching his head and telling him
~~~

he was a good boy. He was trying, but as he stood there his back legs were still trembling.

You read about me using this same technique with Honey. I've received some criticism for these little "walks" in the kennel. Now, if you say you're going to give a dog a treat, I believe you should give them a treat. You don't ever use that as a way of getting them to do something and then fail to make good on the promise. It's just mean. So I understand it when I hear skepticism saying, "How dare you? You told that dog you were going to take them on a walk, and you didn't take them on a walk." I would love to take the dog on a walk, but a dog in this mental state is just not ready to go out on a walk in the neighborhood. You wouldn't go out and run a marathon before getting your running shoes and going for a light jog around the block, you'd work your way up. And if you take that dog on a walk and something terrible happens to the dog, or the dog bites someone or tries to bolt because they are scared–you've put the dog in a really bad situation that wasn't necessary when there were warning signs that the dog wasn't ready. Remember, we have to be these dogs' biggest advocates.

You also have to start small to get the dog to trust you, even just a little. Walking circles in the kennel is a safe initial step to see how the dog reacts to the leash, to the walk, and to you. So it's a valuable part of the process. I know it can be hard on the dog. Sometimes the dog gets excited and thinks, oh great, we're getting out of here, let's go! And then you don't even open the door. That can be disappointing for the dog. I understand the criticism. It's a fair observation. But sometimes you need to take this step if one day these dogs are going to enjoy lots of long walks with a loving family. I have found movement, even in small doses, to be one of the best ways to begin the journey out of trauma. More immediately, it gave me a way to get him moving.

The little walking exercise allowed his muscles to release, which was really helpful. He wasn't so much in his own head now. His body was starting to assert itself again, and dogs' bodies like to move and interact. Plus, I needed him out of that spot at the front of the kennel but didn't want to move him with my hands until he'd moved on his own. He'd already been on the wrong end of too much force. We'd get there, and soon, because the thing a young Mastiff loves but rarely gets–being so large–is to cuddle.

I don't care if you're a 4-pound Chihuahua or a 150-pound Mastiff, every dog is a lap dog. Very few dogs don't like the scoop. And the beauty of it is, if they don't want to stay on your lap, it's not mandatory. More often than not, however, they stay.

Because one thing the scoop allows me to do is rub a dog's head. Really hard. Especially a large puppy with loose skin that I can roll around to get the blood flowing. If you've ever had someone rub your head vigorously, you know that even after they stop it feels great. They've gotten blood circulating right around your brain, and it lets so much tension release. I like to think it lets a little of the trauma in the dogs I meet release, too.

**Moose, the giant puppy, looks small next to his sister, Leia.**

"Moose."

That was the name. He faced me as soon as I repeated it. Credit to Kelly, who also suggested "Ollie," but Moose just seemed to fit better.

Ollie was a cute name, but the Mastiff looked at me when I said "Moose" as if I'd said a name he already knew. And it suited a large dog without adding any note of menace. It's a name that would conjure thoughts of a big, squishy teddy bear. That's the right attitude to keep a dog from being trained into antisocial behavior by the effect of a scary name. And that sealed it.

Moose was taking treats from my fingers now, with no hesitation. And from my open palm, too. That's a huge advancement in trust, when a dog will put their face in your open palm. That told me it was time. But he seemed to know something was up. The little kennel felt extra small when I caught wind of Moose's, let's say, nervous toots. Whatever he'd been eating plus all the anxiety he'd been feeling was evidently wreaking havoc on his stomach–sometimes in this job, you've got to just grin and bear it!

It took some handling and sliding him into position, which he allowed me to do, before I was able to lift him onto my lap and into the scoop. He flopped pretty quickly with the head rubs and ear scratches. I said his name over and over. A great benefit of the scoop is the sense of compression dogs get. For a big, young dog like Moose, not too many people would be picking him up like this (another reason we need more guys helping in shelters–long legs and big laps!) Squeezing him onto my lap let him feel like a puppy again, curled up against someone who's taking care of him. Moose could finally feel safe.

That allows a dog to let their guard down. And boy, did Moose get into the spirit of the scoop. After he settled, Kelly came in and sat with us, and Moose loved it. We read some mail and opened some presents from viewers and just talked while he settled and got head rubs and yawned. As we had all four hands on his wrinkly, velvety coat, naturally a thought came to both of us. We talked about it on the way home and in the days that followed, just how much we'd love to bring Moose to the farm. He'd be a great candidate for rehabilitation, but he's a big young dog who no doubt has a ton of energy, and we were trying to bring along a couple of withdrawn dogs at the time (one of them was Pumpkin, who you'll meet soon). Moose might not be as troublesome as he was described when surrendered—"hyperactive and destructive"—but the energy and size are real, and he'd easily have overwhelmed the dogs we were working with.

The good news is, when we went back to check on Moose a few days later, he was up and moving around. I spent some time with him, and he started approaching me and was happy to take treats. I was so happy to see him in a very different frame of mind than the withdrawn state I'd found him in earlier that week.

Better yet, he had a hold! Holds don't always work out and result in adoptions. But it meant at the very least that someone had seen his video and knew they could give him a better life. And this was a good thing, because Kelly had fallen in love with him, and I told her that if there was no movement on Moose we would figure out a way to help.

A few days later, the hold was no more. Moose had been adopted! And if we were concerned that he wouldn't find somebody who could handle a dog of his size, especially an energetic young one, we needn't have worried.

Two years earlier, Faith and her husband had adopted another Mastiff from the same shelter. Four-year-old Leia was a big girl (who looks even more like Kobe than Moose does), but Faith had lived with Mastiffs since she was a teenager. An owner who knew the breed meant a greater chance of success with Moose. And another dog in the family who could handle him would help, too. Leia still dwarfed him, so Moose could get used to a few ground rules before he outgrew her.

The adoption faced one big hurdle: Leia didn't always get along well with other dogs. The meet and greet would decide Moose's fate. Fortunately, it went fantastically well. Moose went home with his new family and big sister, and even got a fun new name—Kenobi—to keep with the Star Wars theme.

Now imagine being introduced to these two giant Mastiffs, if one's called R.I.P. and the other has an equally scary name, like D.O.A. or something. Do you think people are going to greet those dogs as warmly as they would when they're told they're called Kenobi and Leia? Who isn't going to smile when they hear those two names? And what effect do you think all those happy reactions are going to have on the dogs over time, versus names that make people nervous? Names really do matter.

***Moose with his new forever family.***

The dogs are happy. They nap and play together. Kenobi is gentle and loving with the kids, and any sign that he's afraid of men is gone, as is the effect of his traumatic departure from his old family. The concept of forgiveness would be lost on him, of course, but he knows how good it feels to be treated like a dog who isn't guilty of something terrible, and he's living up to the expectations his new family has of him. Faith says he's a completely different dog than the one she saw online.

Sometimes it takes a while for someone to come along and give us that hug that tells us we're still worth loving and helps the trauma heal. Better late than never. Much better. Just ask the giant puppy we called Moose. What I learned from Moose is that sometimes simply being there for others can help them through trauma or at least reduce the impact of trauma. Flip did this for me when I had a stroke. When you rescue a dog you might be doing that for them, and I know firsthand dogs can do that for all of us.

# CHAPTER 8

# BEAN

# (EVEN WHEN IT HURTS)

SCAN TO LEARN MORE
ABOUT BEAN'S STORY

**Whenever you see a dog in distress, your heart goes out to it. You want to help. But when that dog is a puppy—there's nothing like that feeling. You don't just want to help, you need to help.**

I'd been warned by the shelter staff when I arrived: Something was very wrong with the little Cattle Dog's leg. That's not good for all the obvious reasons—nobody wants to see a puppy in pain. But in a crowded shelter, a badly injured leg could require more resources than the shelter can justify spending on a single animal. And that could mean the saddest of all possible outcomes.

---

There was no mistaking this puppy when I came across his kennel. I found him tucked beneath the front window, where he was barely visible from the hall. All I could see of him was a cute little button nose and face sticking out. I had to laugh. Even the partial view was adorable.

So far so good. But I had only seen his nose and flopped-over ears.

I'd been working with this shelter for so long that they gave me keys to areas the public can't access. That's where they first put the dogs that nobody's sure what to do with when they arrive. Usually, that's because of an injury. When I let myself into the puppy's kennel, the nature of his injury was immediately obvious.

As he hopped out of the corner under the window, I could see that one of his hind legs was just hanging off him, like a wet macaroni noodle. I had to think it was broken in multiple places. The staff had told me he was already on pain meds. Clearly, he needed them.

Not only was the little Australian Cattle Dog certainly in great pain—I knew what that break meant for his odds of getting better. Most shelters just don't have the budget to handle his very probable need for surgery nor the time it would take to make sure he didn't re-injure the leg just by being an energetic puppy. As sad as it would be for everyone involved, euthanasia was a real possibility.

People ask me frequently why veterinarians can't donate some of their time to cases like this. They do! But they can only do so much. And many clinics have been bought up by corporate owners who no longer allow their vets to do so much work for free. It was up to me to find a way to get this puppy the care he so badly needed.

*Meeting Bean at the shelter for the first time.*

As I sat down on the floor with him, he surprised me by putting his head right in my hand. With his button nose, perky ears, and a big black circle around one eye, he looked like a little Muppet. Cattle Dogs have a very particular look. And in this boy's case, it looked like he was smiling. I just wanted to pick him up, but I was too busy trying to discourage him from walking around on that leg. He wasn't deterred. He was a little slow, from the meds, but he had a puppy's curiosity and friendliness.

I could skip my routine approach. He didn't seem scared of me at all. I sat down right away. And before I knew it, he was resting his chin on my leg. He was determined to show me exactly what a brave, charming little guy he could be.

He was also smelling the treats in my back pocket, and after ducking behind me for a moment he emerged with a whole jerky stick in his teeth. Compared to him, the treat stick was so big it made him look like a normal-sized dog carrying a tree branch he'd found in the park. I took it back and broke off smaller, more manageable pieces. He really seemed to want to get on my lap, so I scooped him up, but very slowly. I didn't want to bump that broken hind leg. He wiggled a little, as you'd expect a puppy to do, but then settled in.

He'd been at the shelter two or three days already, dropped off by someone who'd found him wandering near a park. From what we could gather, she'd even kept him for a night, which was an exceptionally kind thing to do, and brought him to the shelter the next day. She said she'd like to keep him, but that break was beyond her capacity to deal with.

The reality of this dog's situation was weighing on me as I sat with him. He probably needed surgery to the tune of $10,000 or more, which the shelter could never afford. I had a thought, though. It was still unannounced, but Flip Farms was almost ready. Aside from being a coffee farm, it was a countryside facility where we could rehabilitate dogs. Profits from our coffee sales could help pay for the care and rehabilitation of dogs–just like the one I was sitting with–until they were ready to be adopted. And, of course, the farm and the coffee were named after one of the all-time greatest rehabilitated rescue dogs!

If I were to imagine the ideal first-ever resident of Flip Farms, you might say he'd just fallen into my lap.

~~~

We'd been working on Flip Farms for years and not telling many people about it. The plan was in place from day one when we bought the property. We wanted to help dogs and grow coffee, but we just weren't sure how to make it all work together. Initially, we were going to wait a few months to announce our ambitions, but I was reminded of something from my childhood about working on farms: Farming takes time. A lot of time. It's a bunch of hurry up and wait. Hurry and get the mulch before the days get too hot so we can retain water and get these plants the nutrients they need. Hurry and pull weed after weed after weed so we can grow without using chemical spray. But then wait for months with not much to do as the plants do what they do, grow.

And financially, farming was a big lift. The cost of growing coffee is steep, because you don't get cherries on your coffee plants that are good enough to sell for the first three to five years. But I figured with all of this time, I could also start building a structure to house the dogs we wanted to rehabilitate. I would build the first one, and then once the coffee was selling and we had a chance to assess how well the structure served its intended purpose, we could finance and build a few more.

That first structure was basically done. Aside from providing a serene location in the rolling hills of North San Diego County, Flip Farms now had its first Quonset hut–a doggy condo–complete with temperature control and soundproofing; we could play relaxing music, and it would be safe and calm, but still stimulating, for a dog whose movement needed to be temporarily restricted while it recovered from injury or illness. I chose a Quonset hut because it's easy enough to assemble with one or two people, and we could choose a budget-friendly option. You've probably seen this sort of structure but didn't realize what it was called. Used often by the military, it's a series of stainless-steel arches that you bolt together making a dome-like shape. If you build end walls on each side with windows and doors, you can make it a small hut, like I did, or larger, right up to a giant airplane hangar.
~~~

Building the first Quonset hut.

Carrying Bean into his first vet appointment.

There were some things Kelly and I knew we wanted the farm to be. One thing we didn't want it to be was a sanctuary, where dogs would spend the rest of their lives. Our goal was for this farm to be a stepping stone. We would take on dogs with the intention of getting them adopted. But until then, they could heal, level out, decompress, learn new things, and be trained; whatever it took for them to be ready for their forever family.

Many people ask me why we don't set up the farm as a nonprofit, and I think that is a fair question. There is nothing wrong with nonprofits, sanctuaries, or however you might structure an organization meant to do good. That being said, I think there is an opportunity for a really fun model that gives back: a small family business that also helps dogs in need. I know that if I had the option to purchase a product at the store from a small family business aligned with doing good, I would support that mission.

Small business is what I know. I'm an entrepreneur and have always found success in doing things a little differently. If I can put all of my energy into something I know how to do, I think I can make a much bigger difference in dogs' lives.

As I sat with the puppy, I imagined ways we could accelerate the completion of the farm so he could recover there. The major obstacle wasn't the unfinished fences (he wouldn't be running around immediately anyway), and the HVAC was being installed in the hut even as we sat there. No, the problem I needed to solve was my wife.

I'd promised Kelly we wouldn't take in any dogs until the farm was completely ready. That meant finishing the fences and the electrical. It also meant drafting a schedule for how we would run the place day to day, complete with kennel cleaning and feeding multiple dogs with different needs. We also needed to find some team members who could help, and all this while we were raising two children, growing coffee, and running the bakeries among other businesses. She was already feeling overwhelmed. It was so much. I'd need a plan. And that plan started with a really cute name for this Cattle Dog that would make it even harder for her to say no.

"We'll have to sell Kelly on it," I told the little dog in my lap. And nothing would sell her on the name like thinking it was her idea.

The mistake I made was thinking she wouldn't figure me out.

With the most adorable injured puppy she'd ever seen dozing sweetly on my lap, I asked Kelly to join me in the kennel. I said I wanted her to help us name him. She suggested Bluey (Blue Heeler is another name for Australian Cattle Dogs), but she had to confess she'd been spending a lot of time immersed in children's entertainment lately. It might not be an awesome suggestion.

I reassured her she was on the right path, saying I'd thought of that name, too. I tried asking Alexis for a suggestion, but she begged out of the discussion. No way was she getting caught in my plot. I offered the name Bean. Kelly said it out loud, trying it on for size. Then I blew it. I made eyes at the camera. Busted.

"You're trying to make this my idea!" she said. "I didn't just meet you today."

Just a hint of me trying to lead her to the name, and she was on to me. And I mean she had *the whole thing* figured out!

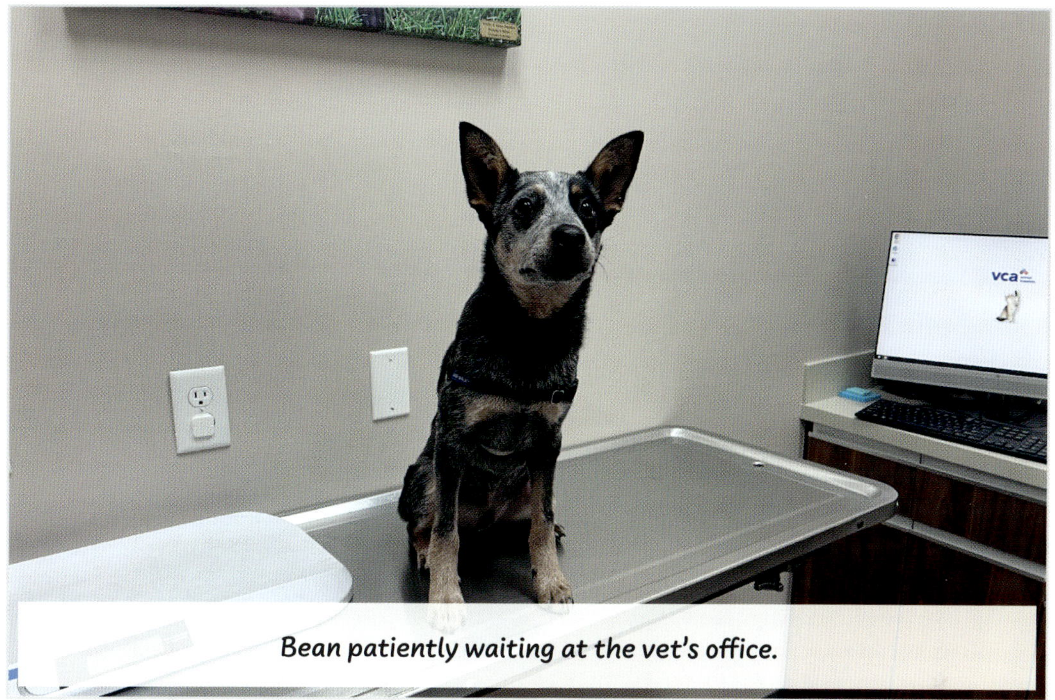

**Bean patiently waiting at the vet's office.**

"You want to name him Bean, after coffee bean. You want to bring him onto Flip Farms."

I laid it on pretty thick about honoring Flip's legacy and doing what was best for the puppy, then dragged Alexis back into it, to weigh in on my plan.

For my grand finale, I carefully scooped the puppy into Kelly's lap.

I might have been in trouble with my wife, but she was in love with this little Bean. I almost had her.

"Dogs like this in shelters with broken legs"–she sighed deeply, stroking the floppy tops of his ears–"it's tough," she said.

He was Bean. And he was coming home to Flip Farms!

---

To get Bean out of the shelter, we adopted him, officially. Our first stop was the vet. That leg was going to need major attention. And quickly. For all we knew, the medication he was on was barely keeping his pain in check. We could only guess whether Bean could even keep the leg. We assumed he'd been hit by a car, though it could have been a number of things. He could have fallen off a balcony, for instance. A break like that isn't likely caused by an abusive owner kicking him—he certainly wasn't behaving like an abused animal. But we had to wonder, if he'd suffered an impact strong enough to do this to his leg, what else could be wrong with him?

Animal Care Services, who had given Macy such extraordinary care while she put on weight, agreed to see Bean at a moment's notice, given his dire condition. Dr. Impett did an immediate workup. The damage to Bean's leg was as bad as we feared. X-rays showed multiple breaks at both the top of his leg and below the knee. Mercifully, the breaks were all that seemed to be wrong with him.

Vets are just like any other doctors: They can't all do everything. We needed to see a specialist. But before leaving for that appointment, Dr. Impett left us with some simple yet profound advice, which I would cling to in the difficult months ahead: "You can always amputate if the specialist is unable to save the leg, but you can't do it the other way around."

I'm so glad she said that, because the specialist we saw next said it made no sense to try to save Bean's leg. We should amputate. As we had seen with Kobe, vets often assume that very expensive surgeries aren't an option for most pet owners; even suggesting surgery to someone who can't afford it can unfairly burden their conscience when there's very little chance of success. We were in a different position, however, as I was confident we would sell lots of Flip Coffee as soon as it launched, and those sales would help pay for the expensive procedures.

When we called to follow up with the specialist about options and details, he was gone and wouldn't be back for a few days. The lead vet tech, however, thought we shouldn't rule out surgery. However, she confirmed that it would be a long and expensive journey. She recommended the leading specialist in the area for leg reconstructive surgery, who fortunately wasn't too far away. And when we met with him, Dr. Sung confirmed that he could definitely try to save the leg, but it would cost $10,000 to $12,000.

I was going back and forth in my heart. I wanted to do what was best for Bean, but what was best was not clear. For one, the funds used to save his leg could do a lot of good for other dogs. It was the same tough question shelters ask when faced with a dog needing expensive

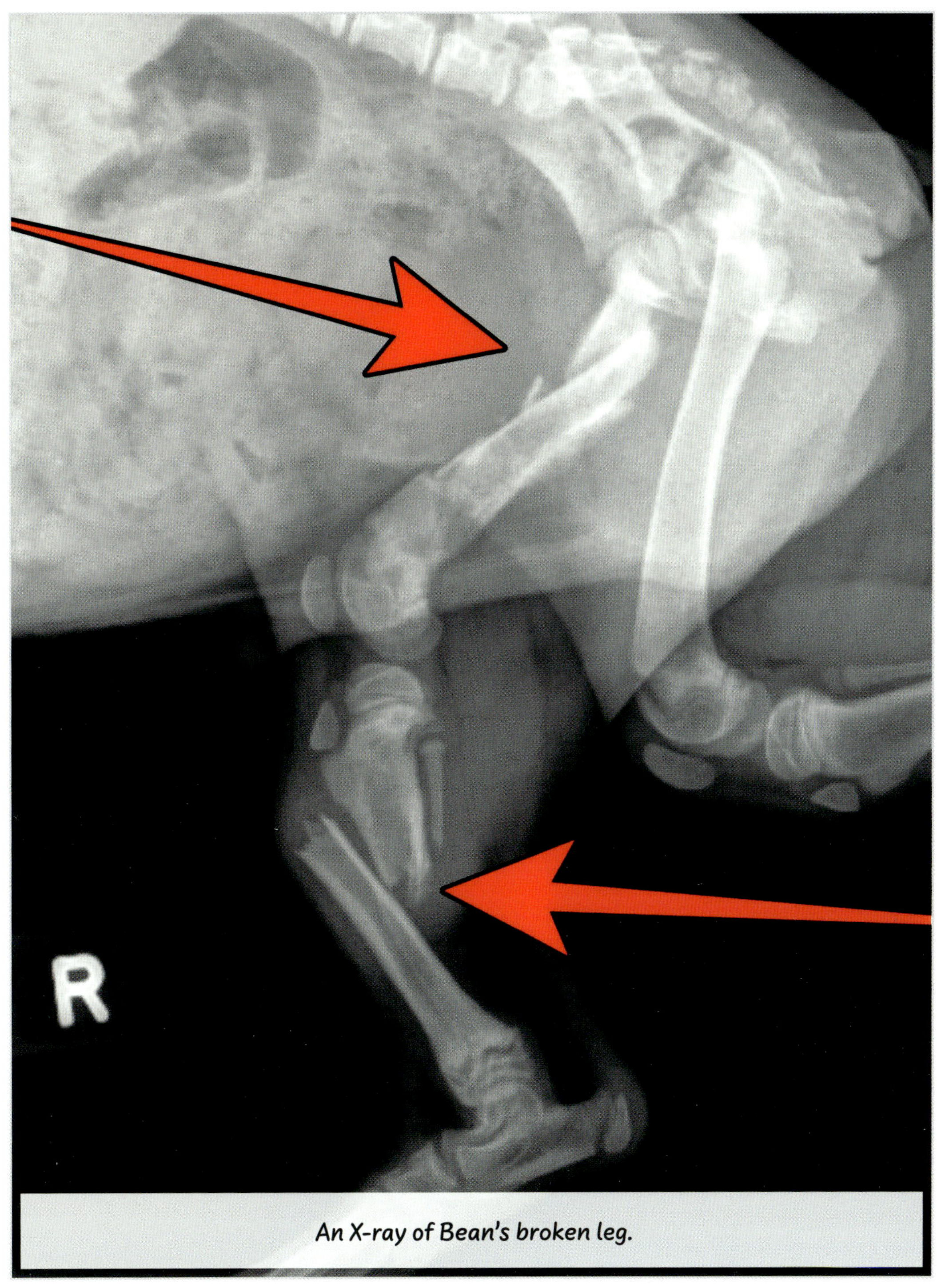


An X-ray of Bean's broken leg.

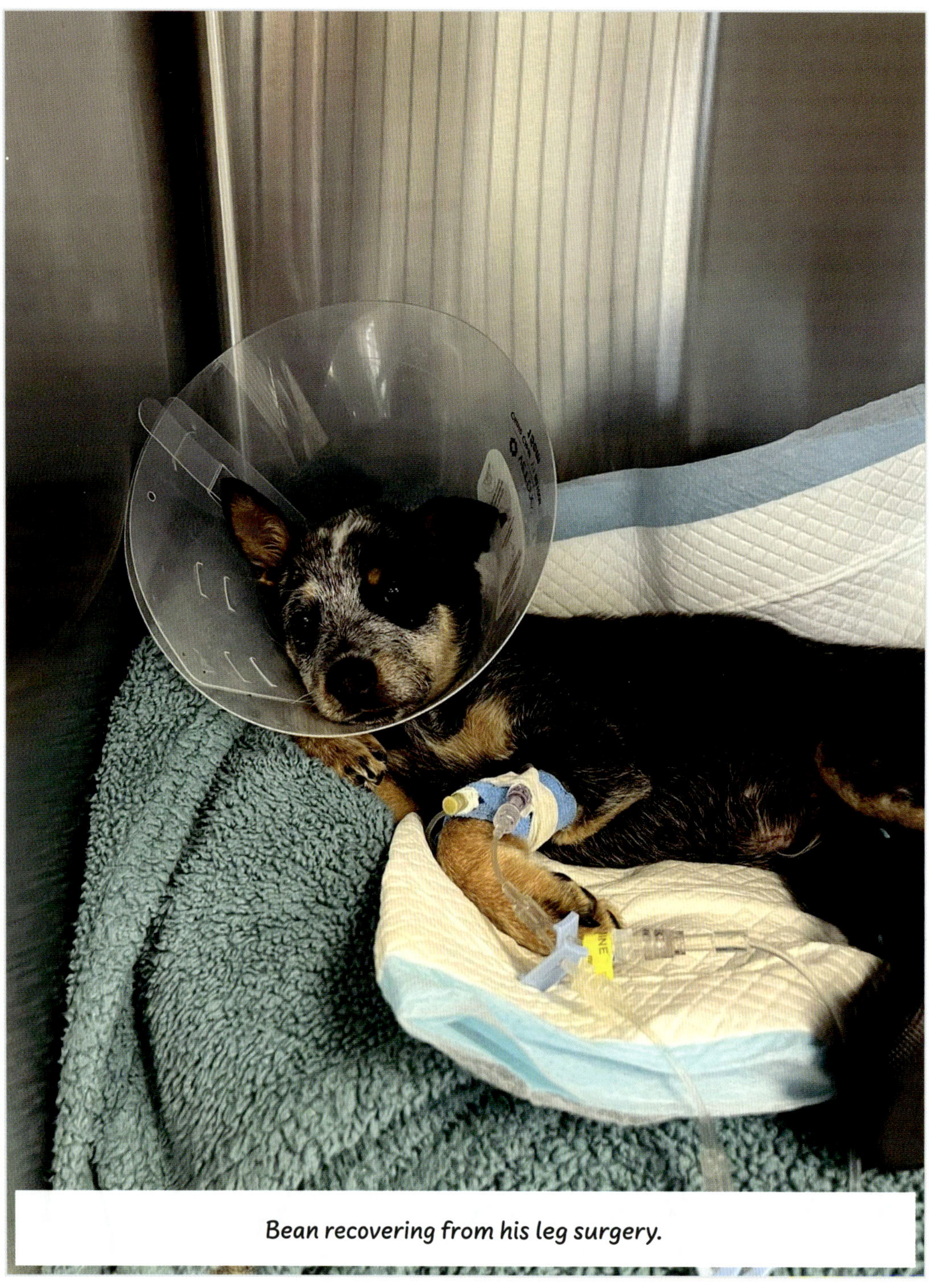

Bean recovering from his leg surgery.

care. I had to wonder, as well, would this process be fair to a puppy? I've met lots of very happy three-legged, even two-legged, dogs. We could just amputate, and he'd bounce back and move on.

But something kept knocking at my heart. This dog and I had come together for a reason. And he had shown me already how tough and resilient he was.

When the specialist detailed the way forward, I didn't even hesitate.

"Do it."

Bean's surgery started at 5 p.m. Scar tissue had formed around the breaks. Removing it added hours to the procedure. It was nearly midnight before Dr. Sung finally stitched him up. From what he had seen, he figured Bean's accident had happened four or five days ago. Some of that time was spent wandering the streets with no painkillers. That's one tough Bean!

The specialist had removed the scar tissue, set the bones, and put plates on them to help the breaks mend. It was time for Bean to recover, which was when Bean's special talent for connecting with people did us all a huge favor. Dr. Impett, the first vet to see Bean after we adopted him, offered to foster him. "There is just something special about this dog," she said. We were thrilled.

This allowed us to wrap up work on Flip Farms while doing our usual million and a half other things–kids, dogs, bakeries, launching Flip Coffee. It also allowed Bean to be around other dogs, though he had to stay still and couldn't socialize much. She sent us lots of photos and we visited often. He was healing nicely and doing great. As he neared the end of his foster time with Dr. Impett, we even did a livestream with her to drum up interest among Bean's many fans in adopting him.

Twenty-four hours after that livestream, the upbeat mood had disappeared. We were rushing Bean to the vet again. As it turned out, he would be the first resident of Flip Farms after all. And those applications to adopt him would have to wait.

The morning after going live with Dr. Impett, she called us with concerning news. Bean was knuckle-dragging. He was pulling his toes across the floor as he walked, and anytime you see that in a dog who is rehabilitating from leg surgery, it's a very bad sign.

One of the plates holding his bones together had broken. The specialist needed to operate again to fix it. If they didn't do it right away, scar tissue would start forming again, and that would mean even more extensive surgery—or, more likely, amputation.

Seeing Bean go back into surgery, I was questioning everything again. Was this the right path for a puppy? This was going to mean another four to six weeks of not being able to move around. He wasn't going to be a puppy much longer. Were we stealing crucial developmental time from him? Who knows what the long-term consequences of a puppyhood spent idling in recovery could be?

People were asking us online, and I was wondering myself, why couldn't we put a cast on him? Or a thicker plate that wouldn't break? So we asked and learned that a cast would prevent his joints from twisting in the correct way as they continued to develop, which could limit his leg motion as an adult. Also, we would have to replace the cast nearly every week. He was still growing, and a cast that fit him one week might not fit the next. As for the plates, a plate that's too thick wouldn't work because the bones, cartilage, and muscle in his leg needed to grow around the metal, which couldn't happen if it was too thick.

We brought him to the farm. At the Quonset hut, we could hear the birds in the morning and sit basking in the sun pouring through its big window. Outside, the rows of green coffee trees bloomed with clusters of cherries. I don't know if Bean appreciated the view as much as we did, but it was peaceful, which he needed to help him rest. We played spa music during the night to drown out any coyotes howling in the distance or any other strange noises that might prevent him from feeling safe and sound. Kelly and I visited the hut only on a very regimented schedule. We would feed him, let him go outside for a quick bathroom break, then give him some snuggles and put him back in his crate in the hut. If we spent any more time with him, he would become too playful and risk breaking another plate. He needed to rest quietly, as much as his puppy's heart wanted to run, run, run.

Let me tell you, tearing ourselves away from Bean several times a day was one of the hardest things ever. I could see in his eyes that he didn't understand why we would leave. We had some team members start taking on some of his scheduled visits, partly so he would become accustomed to other people, which would be essential if he was going to be adopted, but partly so we could take a mental break from having to leave this cute little Bean over and over again.

On the other hand, the great thing about Bean's regimented schedule was how it built up anticipation for every visit. Kelly and I were all excited to join him at the hut for even a few minutes at a time. He was on sedation and pain medication, but Bean's boundless energy made it hard to tell the difference. And his vibrant personality always leaned towards happiness, no matter the pain or whatever else was happening around him. Life hadn't been easy so far, but he was ready to make the best of it.

That remained true even when something else went wrong.

I didn't know what I was seeing, but I knew that I was seeing it.

When you work with rescue dogs, you develop an eye for small problems that might become big ones. A dog becomes melancholy, or they're just slow to get up, or they have potty problems. None of this was happening with Bean, but his

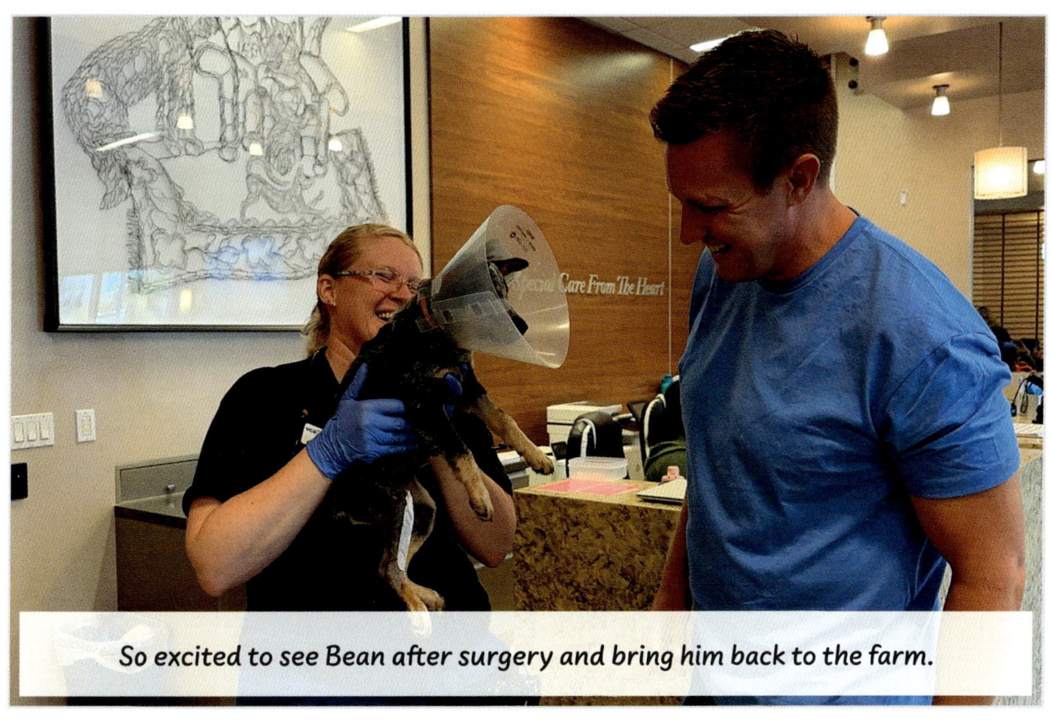


**So excited to see Bean after surgery and bring him back to the farm.**

eyes had turned glassy. He seemed happy as a clam, still eating. But something was off. Four weeks after the surgery to fix his plates, I was seeing something in his face–a look that said, "Help me."

Bean's recovery had been going great–again. And we were just days away from the checkup that we expected would clear him for adoption. But here we were again, rushing him to the specialist, Dr. Sung. We were worried maybe an infection had set in from the last surgery. I've seen that happen before to a bulldog I was rehabilitating. Bean wasn't knuckle-dragging again, so whatever was happening to him must be new. I couldn't figure it out, but my best guess was that something was off from his most recent surgery.

Looking at the new X-rays, the vet couldn't imagine why Bean wasn't passed out from the pain. Outside of his glassy eyes, he wasn't showing any signs of discomfort–let alone a diaphragmatic hernia. Bean had developed a tear in his abdominal cavity that allowed his intestines to move into his chest. The vet was surprised there was enough space left around Bean's lungs for him to breathe.

I was beating myself up for not having noticed anything wrong

***Bean hanging in the shade by the coffee trees.***

Bean enjoying the morning sun.

before this. But Bean had been in confinement with very limited activity. His lack of motion had slowed the tear. There had been no signs to see. There was, however, a lesson in this: When you foster dogs with big problems, you're going to make at least a few small mistakes. Just provide love and safety and the necessities of life, and pay close attention to them. You'll get better at the rest.

As it turns out, hernias like Bean's are not uncommon in cases of severe blunt-force trauma. A massive impact can cause widespread internal damage, as we'd suspected might have happened to Bean–the tear just hadn't been noticeable yet during his first surgery, when the doctor thought everything but the leg was fine.

I was worried. The total bill for Bean's recovery was now around $40,000, but thanks to so many of his believers supporting us and purchasing coffee, I knew in time we would be able to cover the cost. But the cost to Bean? He was going to have to return to weeks of confinement. Could all that isolation have a lasting effect on a young dog's mental health? Could our decision not to amputate from the beginning have set him up for problems throughout the rest of his life?

After Bean went in for surgery, I made a big mistake. I googled his condition. The likelihood of success for Bean's surgery was anywhere between 20 and 80 percent. That really narrowed it down! What if we'd brought him this far, only to lose him? The hernia surgery was usually successful, but Bean's condition had been going on for a while, undetected and slowly getting worse. All we could do was wait.

Some good news arrived in the meantime. While Bean was still unconscious, the doctor checked his leg. It was 100 percent! He let us know before the main procedure was completely done, which left us in a weird spot. We were celebrating the completely healed leg, but poor Bean wasn't even out of the woods yet with his hernia procedure. This happy moment could take a terrible turn the next time the specialist came out of the surgery.

Happily, it wasn't much longer before we learned that the hernia had been stitched up without complication. The surgery was a success.

Bean was still a puppy, but already he was a testament to an incredible breed. The Australian Cattle Dog is a whole lot of energy, tenacity, and loyalty packed into a body that's rarely more than forty pounds. At the time we met Bean, he was only a fraction of that. When I think of the pain he must have been feeling and how charismatic and friendly he was, regardless—he really is tough as nails. Just one more example of why dogs are so amazing.

So how do you let a perfect little dog like Bean go? It's not easy. He would have been the ideal dog for us and the farm. But Kelly and I made a commitment to each other that the farm would be just a chapter in the fairytale of many dogs' lives.

Of course, we had another reason not to keep Bean—a reason who weighed about a hundred pounds. We tried a meet and greet with Kobe and Bean at the house, but Bean's energy was not meant for small spaces or blind dogs with bad hearts. Kobe's anxiety went through the roof. That wasn't going to work.

Besides, we'd broken our promise not to keep one foster—and Kobe was making the most of his extra years. But he would always live with us at home and need special care. The farm was for a different purpose. Once healed from his hernia surgery, Bean wouldn't need special care any longer.

We had some wonderful applicants hoping to adopt him. One couple, Andrew and Shirley, brought their corgis, and they got along fine with Bean. But by then another Australian Cattle Dog had arrived at the shelter. She was an adult named Cookie. Recognizing that Bean had become one of the channel's biggest stars, Andrew and Shirley instead adopted her, renaming her Kona, as a nod to the big guy from Hawaii who helped bring them together. (I was honored.)

That left Bean available to another very special applicant. One who seemed just right, because she had been there from the beginning.

~~~

We had finally clarified the story of Bean's arrival at the shelter—or at least as much as we ever would. The day before he showed up at the shelter, a woman named Stephanie had found him partially hidden in the weeds along the side of a main street. She thought he might be a rabbit, he was so small. She slowed down in traffic to get a better look. Other drivers started honking at
~~~

*Hanging with Bean in his Quonset hut.*

her, so she pulled to the side of the road, got out, and picked up the tiny puppy. There was a park nearby, and she wondered if he'd gotten away from someone there. She waited, just in case, but nobody came looking for him.

She called Animal Control and an officer took him to see a vet, who confirmed the seriousness of his injury. But it was late in the day, and so the officer brought him home for a night before surrendering him to the shelter. Meanwhile, Stephanie let the shelter know she wanted to help, to do more, but wasn't able because of the likely cost associated with Bean's injury.

Stephanie couldn't forget about the little Cattle Dog. She continued to check in with the shelter and us every step of the way, and she always let us know she would love to adopt him if we would be willing to choose her. So we reached out to Stephanie. There had been so many delays with Bean's surgeries and recovery. Was she still interested in adopting him? She was more than interested. She'd been following his story online and had never given up hope that maybe she'd see him again.

Dogs hold a place in their hearts for people who show them love when they need it—and even save them. And make no mistake, if Stephanie hadn't ignored all those other drivers and pulled over to collect Bean from the side of the road, he'd have soon starved or run into coyotes or a car. She'd saved him then, and she was about to save him again.

We set up a meet and greet. It went great, and we all thought it made good sense for Stephanie to adopt Bean. She came back for another visit, and I told Bean, "It's going to happen. This is going to be your new mom!" When she came to the farm to pick him up for the adoption, he was bouncing with excitement. He remembered her from her visits, but I believe he remembered her from the worst day of his life, too. Because thanks to Stephanie, it was also the day his life turned around and pointed him toward an amazing future—a future he never failed to face with a smile.

~~~

I've fostered many dogs over the years. Every so often, moments will come out of nowhere and I'll mourn their departure from my life. But that mourning is balanced by joy. They found the loving homes they deserved. And even for those dogs who have since passed on, crossed the rainbow bridge, for them life got
~~~

Bean reuniting with his new mom, Stephanie.

*The best Bean there ever was.*

a lot better before it was done, thanks to people who opened their homes and shared their love.

I have sent messages to Kelly in moments when I miss Bean, saying I think we made a mistake, and we should have kept him. But that's not at all true, even if it sometimes feels like it. I can't let missing him overshadow the fact that we don't do this for us, we do it for the dogs (we do get photos–it was part of the adoption agreement!) Nor can I let it overshadow the great gift that Bean gave us, one that lives on in our hearts even in his absence.

I learn from every dog I help and foster. They've helped me become the man I am today. Without Flip and Kobe and Bean, and all the others, I would certainly be lost. But the thing I learned most from Bean was that even when he was going through the worst pain and loneliness, when he could barely even move forward physically, he met us all with a smile on his face. I've been medically incapacitated at times in my life. I don't know that I can say I met those moments with as much bravery as that little Cattle Dog. Relishing the moment, even when it hurt, he was always happy to see me, happy to get the treats he was getting, the food he was eating, and the safety and care he was receiving.

He had no reason to trust anyone. But he did. He will forever be our first dog on Flip Farms. We will carry him with us, forever and always. It's community that kept him going; the love and support of all the many people who were part of his story. He could feel it. He could feel and understand love. And it certainly saved his life.

VOYAGER

# CHAPTER 9

# PUMPKIN

## (FERAL AND BACK)

SCAN TO LEARN MORE
ABOUT PUMPKIN'S STORY

**I can usually make a difference with a withdrawn dog within a sitting, sometimes two. But in one of the most severe cases I've ever dealt with, I knew we wouldn't see a turnaround in the dog without months of rehabilitation. It was painfully clear to me as I entered his kennel that in that moment, I was this dog's monster, the last thing he wanted to see entering the tiny space separating him from the terrifying world outside.**

This dog, who I immediately started calling Pumpkin, wasn't just frightened. Not even "traumatized" captured the state he was in, although trauma of some sort had most likely played a part in his condition. Whatever had happened to that dog before arriving at the shelter had taken him to a place much deeper than fear–one I'd seen before.

I found the dog in the sallyport. He was auburn-colored with a puffy coat. I couldn't tell what breed he was, but he was certainly a handsome dog. He hadn't been letting anyone near, and the shelter wouldn't expose him to the public in this condition. He hadn't even been through health-check, despite being on his third day in the shelter.

I rarely ask for a dog's story so early after sitting down with them, since it can taint my own impression of the dog's behavior. But this dog was one of the most unreactive I'd ever seen. No movement, no signs of aggression, no desire for touch, nothing. He was just lying against the side wall of a small kennel, facing the door with his head up.

These are always the hardest cases, sometimes the scary ones, as I'd seen with Casper. With so little behavior to work with, which also usually means a lot of fear in the dog, I just can't read whether the dog might lash out. If there was a history of anything that might help and keep the dog and me out of danger, I figured I'd better learn about it now.

I said the dog hadn't moved since I sat down. That wasn't exactly true. He'd had a movement when I opened his door. And it wasn't just bad timing on my part, showing up just as a dog who has nowhere else to go made a mess of himself. I was the reason he defecated on the floor. He could not control himself, so intense was his fear. So I wasn't going to risk touching the dog until I had some background. His bushy tail was tucked so securely around his hindquarters, and he had been so resistant to handling, that the staff hadn't been able to determine yet that he was a boy.

I was sweating as I sat with him. We were facing opposite directions, so I wouldn't scare him with eye contact. But we were still very close to each other. It was a hot day in Southern California, but anxiety has a way of transferring in close quarters. When you allow yourself to be vulnerable to the dog, you end up sharing their feelings. And this guy was feeling pure fear.

I tried putting a few pieces of jerky on the floor. He sniffed but didn't bite. He was panting and drooling, visibly tired from lack of sleep and being stuck in such an anxious state. I was hopeful that we could still turn the dog around during this visit, but I could see progress wouldn't come without patience.

Kelly learned he had been found on a nearby reservation. It wasn't part of the shelter's catchment area, but Animal Control was asked to assist because this situation and the dog's condition exceeded any expertise available on the reservation. A few more conversations around the shelter led us to understand that he had most likely been severely abused. That would go some way to explaining his withdrawn behavior. But Moose was a case of a dog reacting to angry or violent treatment. I was beginning to suspect something more in Pumpkin's case.

We later spoke with Officer Servantes of Animal Control, who had collected the dog from the ranger station at the reservation. He had rejected a leash when she'd tried to take him in her truck, so she'd had to use the catch pole, which had led to him snarling. That's not a surprise. The catch pole is a last-ditch sort of tool for collecting a dog. It's unpleasant, but still better than the alternative of letting him run wild around speeding cars and packs of hungry coyotes.

Office Servantes told us of a curious thing the dog had done when she'd approached: "When I first met him, he kind of puffed up like a cat. I've never, ever seen that before." I'd never seen that body language either. This dog was definitely different. Which led us to a question that became a bit of an obsession in our time with Pumpkin: What kind of dog was he?

His kennel card said a Shar Pei mix. It was a guess, of course. I doubted it, as Pumpkin has a long pointy snout, totally unlike a Shar Pei. Kelly had an AI photo scanner on her phone that helped determine breeds by taking a dog's picture, and it pointed to Pumpkin being either a Korean Jindo dog or a Carolina dog. It didn't matter much yet. We were a long way from any

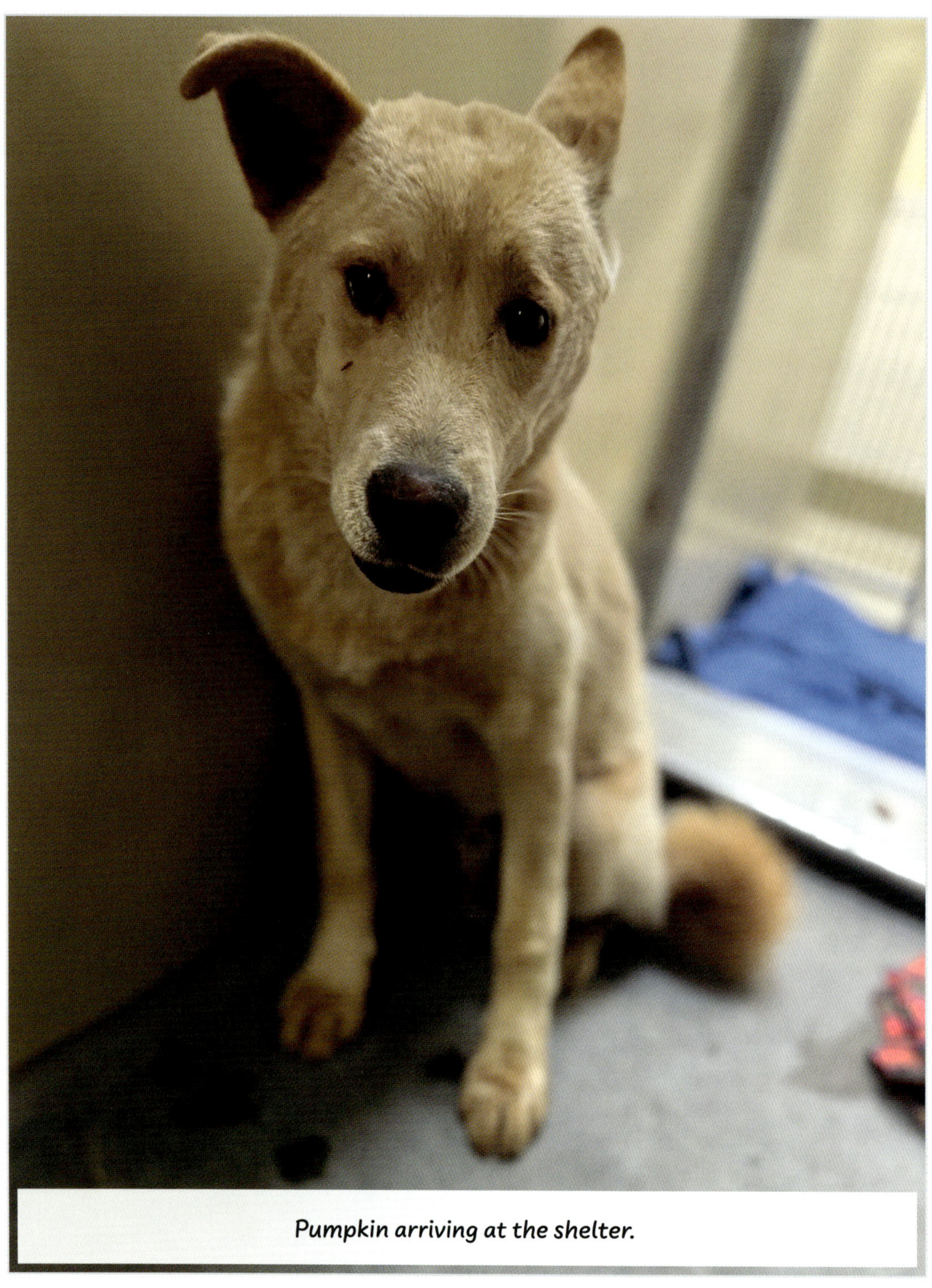

*Pumpkin arriving at the shelter.*

sort of training that might benefit from knowing this dog's breed.

The information card also said he was a senior dog. That surprised me. He didn't seem old, but he was filthy and smelled terrible, so it was hard to get much of a read on anything about him. And once I'd gotten a look at his teeth, I could see they were stained and dirty. Senior dogs are a lot more delicate. They take a lot more time, care, and dedication than other dogs. I supposed this would be the case with Pumpkin, as well.

I tried petting his flank. No reaction, which was good. He didn't snarl at me or try to bite. I touched his ears while giving him some positive affirmations. His ears were adorable. One stayed up while the top of the other flopped down. When I said, "Good dog," both ears perked up, and he glanced briefly in my direction. That felt like I'd found some traction.

"The good news," I said to him, "is that I'm here, and we're going to get through this together."

I was chalking up the bad odor to being just a fact of life when working

**Meeting Pumpkin for the first time.**

with a frightened older dog. It was a little deflating, though, because I thought we'd been getting somewhere with Pumpkin. Maybe he wasn't reacting as well as I thought. Then Kelly pointed out that the dog next door was the real culprit. Phew.

Pumpkin was responding to pets on the head, even vigorous ones. And neck rubs. I tried another treat in front of his nose. Still nothing. I wanted to scoop him, but I was hesitant. I needed more feedback to be sure he would accept my handling him. Pumpkin gave me the sign I was looking for when he stretched his neck in my direction, a clear signal that more pets would be very welcome! I got into some heavy head rubs, and Pumpkin started to melt.

It was October. Pumpkin was the right name for the season–or nickname, I had to remind myself. Pumpkin would get adopted! I promised him. And a soft name would help prospective adopters see what a cute, kind dog they could take home and give a new lease on life. So after a very short discussion, we stuck with Pumpkin.

That new lease on life was going to need some help. So I scooted backward across the floor to be closer to him, got my arms around him, and scooped him up on my lap. Pumpkin was rigid. He lay like a stiff plank across my crossed legs until I could pull up his hindquarters and get him into a bit of a curl.

With my crooked elbow acting like a leash under Pumpkin's chin, I held him close, let him feel the compression that some frightened dogs find so comforting, and kept him in place long enough to let the physical contact produce a sense of security. I stretched my fingers over his scalp and gave him another good head rub, and he started to soften up. He still wouldn't take a treat, but he was accepting all the affection I could offer.

When I'd picked him up, he left a little something on the floor. I was going to need to change my clothes when we finished our visit with Pumpkin, that was for sure. But who cares? To give a dog in misery some hint of a way forward with a few moments of love like this–potentially lifesaving love!–you just deal with the feces and the stink and the dirt. I can always take a bath, no big deal. But Pumpkin's future was a lot more limited if we didn't get him started on our journey together. That's a big enough deal to put up with a few stains and bad smells. And as it turned out, he didn't go to the

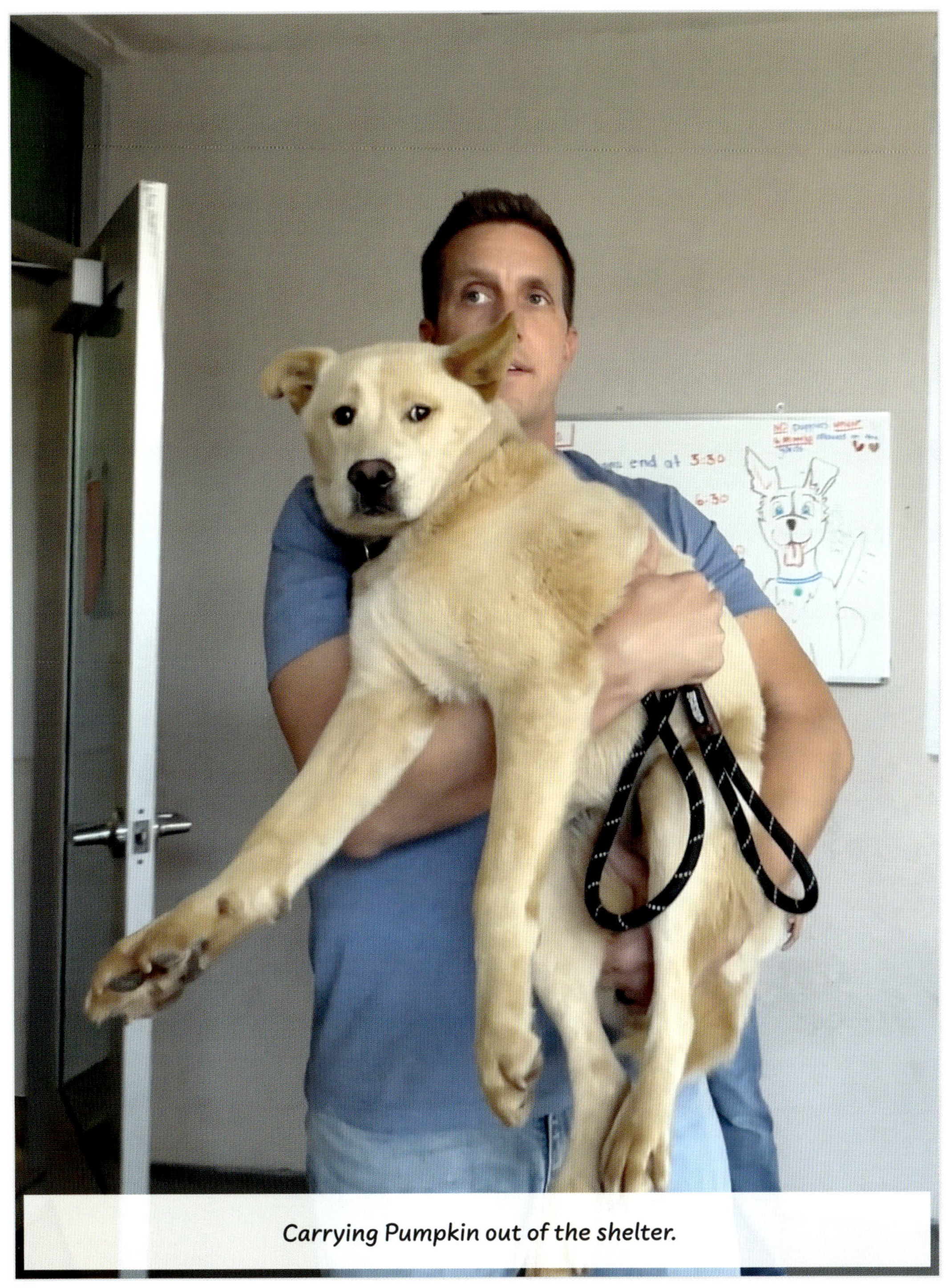


*Carrying Pumpkin out of the shelter.*

bathroom on me. It was just dirt and who knows what else coming off his coat.

---

"We knew he was a puppy!" Kelly said.

We were back at the shelter about a week later. We found Pumpkin worse than we'd left him. He was in isolation now, still too withdrawn to be viewed by the public for adoption.

Standing out in the courtyard, one of the vet techs on staff, Dallas, filled me in on the past week. Pumpkin had gone through health-check after Dallas had carried him to the exam space. She got his vaccinations into him, but he sat tucked in a corner the whole time, completely shut down while Dallas did her thing.

His teeth looked old, but that could have been nutrition. When I had scooped him, I'd noticed he was a bit thin and frail, like you'd expect a senior dog to be. And the filth caked in that puffy fur didn't exactly let his youth shine through. The shelter staff have a lot of experience guessing the ages of

**Pumpkin taking his first ride to the farm.**

dogs with no history, so I'm usually inclined to go with their estimate. But Pumpkin had that round puppy face. I had a sense he was younger than they thought.

"Can I pull him?" I asked Dallas. We'd need a few days to get the Quonset hut ready for him, but I wanted Pumpkin at Flip Farms. He'd never turn himself around in a shelter environment. And I was beginning to understand why. But more on that in a moment.

I went inside to sit with Pumpkin for a few minutes before we left. He shrunk away from me when I came close, but I sat right in front of him so if he remembered me he wouldn't have to go far to initiate more contact. I was giving him head rubs as soon as I sat down.

"Remember I made a promise to you that it's going to be okay?" I said to him. He looked so forlorn there in solitary, so frightened for so long. In some ways, it was even sadder to see him like this now that we knew he was only eight months old. The bouncy puppy energy that should have had him tearing around like a wild thing was nowhere to be seen.

I lifted his front paws onto my thigh. I didn't have time to wait until he was ready for a full scoop, but I wanted him to remember what he'd felt like during our earlier visit, relaxed on my lap. Remarkably, he was still refusing treats. I promised to bake him a pumpkin pie, because he looked like a little pumpkin, and I thought it was likely he would be with our family for Thanksgiving.

As I sat with him this time, Kelly and I wondered about whether another dog would be helpful to mentor him. We didn't have anyone in that job at the farm, currently. But the shelter tried it in the yard. Pumpkin wasn't crazy about the idea and mostly stayed pressed up against the chain-link fence of the little enclosure. He didn't lash out, though, and the other dog wasn't put off by him and trotted around the yard wagging its tail. Staff kept the trial meet and greet brief, just to learn how Pumpkin would handle another dog. Not terrible.

When we returned to pick up Pumpkin, he greeted me by peeing on the kennel floor. He couldn't get rid of me that easily! It might have seemed a bit odd to see me do what I did next with a dog of Pumpkin's size (Pumpkin is about 35 pounds), but I lifted him out of the kennel and carried him down the hall. Maybe he sensed life really was going to get better now, because he pressed his head against my shoulder for the walk, like he was saying, "Okay, I'm trusting you. Please don't fail me."

Mel the groomer was waiting for us. "He's got an old soul," she said to me, as she lathered him up. She was as surprised as any of us to learn how young Pumpkin was. "He's got a couple of different smells that are coming to me," she added. Pumpkin was going to need work, but first and foremost, he needed to get cleaned up.

Mel did her usual great job of keeping the dog calm as she rubbed in the suds and warm water, and gave him pets to reassure him as she blow-dried his coat. I'm so thankful for Mel and the love and relief she brings to all the animals she cares for. When she was done, an orange bandana matched his auburn coat just beautifully (and seasonally!) It was time to head to the farm.

With us, Pumpkin would get the time he needed. He needed a lot of it. I realized, the more I saw of him and learned about him, what was going on inside his head. I knew through experience. I'd had the opportunity to help with hoarding case dogs and feral dogs. I know their behavior, and I recognized that Pumpkin had gone feral.

You wouldn't be alone if you thought a feral dog is a dog that's lived their entire life outside, without human companionship and guidance, fending for itself like a wolf or coyote. But even a domesticated dog's behavior and mentality can regress very quickly. If dogs find themselves suddenly unprotected, nature will do its job and help them become very fearful of anything that might harm them, including humans. They can regress to feral within months. After that happens, it can take years to bring them back, if they ever come back. I've noticed that even rescued and re-domesticated feral dogs never completely lose that feral instinct. It's as if once they've tapped that side of their nature, that ability to live wild, no matter how much care we give them they can never completely shut it off.

If you've ever been through something traumatic or been discriminated against or abused, even if you feel you've healed a hundred percent, you have that scar that will never go away. You will always know it's there. Sometimes that's a very powerful thing, a reminder of the strength that allowed you to come through whatever it was, and you might guard it, like a treasure, a reminder of who you can be. Sometimes it sets you back.

*Pumpkin taking his first steps at the farm.*

Cozying up on the couch at Christmastime.

To help a feral dog or a hoarding-case dog, it helps to know from the beginning that you'll never make that scar disappear. What they need from you is to show them how to be a dog, to guide them back. You need to remind them that it's okay to be loved, it's okay to trust and give your love in return. Teaching a dog to do that again—or maybe for the first time—is a lengthy process, a process that many people are not prepared to do. You might be tempted to think a dog will recover within a couple of weeks. That's not how it's going to happen with a feral dog. It takes time, but you can do it.

I learned how in my early days with dog rescue.

I learned from Blossom, who was rescued from the house of a terrible hoarding case. She lived with 160 other dogs in a single room, if you can call that living. The room was no larger than a kid's bedroom. The dogs were packed in so tight they couldn't sit on the floor, so they sat on other dogs. They ate from a dog food bag the owner just threw into the room. After getting out of there, it took Blossom six months just to sit on my lap, and she fared better than most of the others. Of the 160 dogs, I would say about half had to be euthanized—they were so far gone physically or mentally. The other half were dispersed to rescues across the nation.

Blossom was about 25 pounds and looked like Lady from *Lady and the Tramp*, and she had the permanent puppy eyes look that she gave you all day every day. I tried to shower her with love and hugs. I learned very quickly that wasn't going to work. It was like trying to help someone who was scared of spiders by locking them in a room full of cobwebs. I didn't know that. Looking back, sometimes I feel bad about my mistakes. But I'm also so happy that I made those mistakes, because she and I got through it together, which allowed me to help another dog named Homer.

Homer was a feral dog found with wire wrapped around his abdomen. He was running in the wild for months and months, and it finally took traps to catch him. Not harmful traps, mind you, but traps that would catch him because no human could get close to him. He wouldn't let anyone near. It took him 10 months to come around. Now he's the happiest boy ever. I'm so lucky that Kelly's dad and mom adopted him and I get to see him on a regular basis. But he's still a dog that few people would understand. He hides from most people, ducks and rolls on a walk through the neighborhood, and slinks around corners. I think most people would think he is broken and try to return him to a shelter, but my in-laws love him because they know his story and who he is. If he does come up to you to say hello and looks at you with his little smile, you will feel truly special.

I'm so thankful to Blossom and Homer–and all the other dogs who came home with me not because I was an expert, but because I was willing to open my home and heart and learn. Thanks to them, I was now in a position to pay it forward by helping Pumpkin.

~~~

When I entered the Quonset hut where Pumpkin was staying on the farm, I got down on my hands and knees and army-crawled in so I wouldn't frighten him. I talked about Moose being afraid of men, which he wasn't exactly, despite the rough treatment we think he suffered after the incident with the cat. Most of the time when we think dogs are afraid of men, that isn't really the case. But with Pumpkin, it was absolutely the case. He was scared of men. Maybe that was from abuse, as we were told at the shelter. We had no way to know, in the end. But thanks to everything taught to me by the dogs that came before Pumpkin, I had a way of working through his fear with him. When I would walk in (even after three weeks at the farm), he would often wet himself, unless I got down and army-crawled in, slowly. When Kelly or any of the women on the team walked in, he was still reserved but didn't make a mess.

We are still trying to determine what breed Pumpkin is. He has a spotted tongue, which can happen in individuals of a dozen or so different breeds. Shar Peis and Chows have purple tongues, so a mix might result in spots. Akitas are about the right size and appearance for Pumpkin to be the offspring of one and something else. Akitas can have purple on their tongues as well. We are planning a DNA test to narrow it down, as knowing what his genetic inclinations are–if he's a protection breed, a herding breed, or a couch potato–could help us plan the right activities for his rehabilitation. But mostly we're just curious. He's such a neat dog! And completely adorable. I'm head over heels in love with him.

Not that I'm necessarily his favorite in return. Looking ahead to the day when he can be adopted, Kelly and I did a livestream video from his hut.
~~~

Pumpkin having fun playing fetch.

It was the first time I'd walked into the hut that he didn't wet himself. So that's progress—for me, at least. But then Kelly sat in front of his crate and he hopped right out of it, wagging his tail and tucking his head against her face while she gave him neck rubs. He jawed on a jerky stick but didn't eat it. Then he jumped on a dog bed, closer to me. I could give him head rubs, but he wasn't quite as comfortable receiving them as he'd been with Kelly. His fear of men continued. Maybe men seem scary. But there are good men who will treat him kindly. He deserves to know that, at least.

Pumpkin's journey has just started. At the time we broadcast from his hut, he'd been with us for a month. There's one endearing thing he did that I'd never seen a dog this far withdrawn do. He loved to touch the top of his head to the top of mine. He got a little nervous sometimes when I petted him or when I walked up to him outside. He wouldn't always take treats from me. But if I put my head down, he somehow figured that little head bump was a

*Pumpkin's favorite month of the year is October.*

safe way to express his affection. It was the cutest thing. I didn't understand it, but I welcomed it. It brings me to tears when I think about it. That was his way of communicating. His way of saying, "I'm trying. You're making progress. Don't be offended if I don't accept what you're giving me right now. I will come around."

When we were going live with our community, at one point I was reaching for a bag of treats and accidentally knocked over a little camera. The noise wasn't too loud, but the thump it made startled Pumpkin enough for him to hustle back into his crate. The retreat didn't last long, though. The crinkle of the treat bag brought him right back out. I handed him the stick and he took it, then went back to his crate to eat it.

I talked a little more as we continued, about his eating, about keeping him on a leash outside because feral dogs tend to be very good at slipping out of their leads. As a feral, Pumpkin had me working harder than I would with just about any other dog. But that's okay. It's what we built Flip Farms to do.

Pumpkin ventured out again as I was talking. Just over my shoulder, he was pressing his head against Kelly's chin, and she was sinking her fingers deep into his coat around his neck and shoulders, every second making him more and more comfortable with contact. He was looking as happy as we could hope for him to be in these early days of his rehabilitation. He stepped forward towards me, sniffing for treats, I think. He sniffed my ear a few times. Then he gave me a quick little slurp.

We were heading into November, Thanksgiving season. I have so much to be thankful for. A moment like this with a dog like Pumpkin–on a long, difficult journey, but moving forward with the determined spirit that makes us so grateful to have dogs in our lives–that is most definitely one of them.

At the time of the writing of this book, Pumpkin is still with me. He runs up to me like a normal dog and gets excited about treats; I even heard him bark once over the last four months he's been here. He doesn't know it yet, but he's almost ready to be adopted. He will likely always be reserved. To this day, he still reminds himself that he should be scared and reserved. You can see it in his movements. He'll be having a good time and enjoying himself then he remembers he should be scared and quickly retreats. But those moments are happening less and less, and I hope one day they are few and far between. By the time you're reading this you should be able to check up on an amazing Pumpkin Pupdate and his DNA test results!

**Pumpkin enjoying a walk on the farm.**

Pumpkin almost ready to find his forever home.

# CHAPTER 10

# LIFE IS BETTER WITH DOGS

**People in our community often ask me how I started sitting with dogs. Some want to know about the beginnings of the channel and my work with dogs, which I described at the start of this book. And you read how sitting with my own dogs helped inspire my technique of literally sitting with dogs in shelters. But what many people want to know is how they can help shelter dogs too. I think it's great that they want to do this.**

The good news? You *can* do this.

Everyone is different, so they can help shelter dogs (and cats!) in their own way. You don't have to do it the way I do it. But to answer the big question of "How can I help?" I'm going to start at the beginning, so maybe my story can inspire you or inspire some brand-new ideas with other creative people who have some room to spare in their hearts.

---

As I've said, I grew up poor. We didn't have anything. I honestly believe those difficult early years played a big role in my connection with dogs.

My mom was perfect and is perfect in every way. She always made sure we had bellies full of food. She was great at making chili and stretching soup to last a while. We didn't have meat in our chili, though, just a lot of beans—beans, beans, beans. To this day I hate beans. And Fridays were for leftovers. Of course, all the best food had been eaten, so it was leftovers of the leftovers. I still hate leftovers the same way I hate beans. But I never went to school or bed hungry thanks to my mom doing whatever it took to provide for us. To my mother, I was always good enough, I was always loved, and I always had a full belly. Without her I would not be the man I am today.

We were a churchgoing family, and the church would drop off groceries for us. People would take turns bringing us food. This was in part because my dad was not like my mom. He always thought we were fine so long as we had two outfits to wear. I had a neon green shirt and another old shirt with stains on it. I was supposed to switch off from one day to the next, but that stained shirt looked terrible. Other kids would tease me about wearing the neon green shirt so often. I'd try to cover for it, saying, "Oh, I have a bunch of these because I love neon green. It's my favorite color."

Pants were a problem too. One time I ripped mine climbing the flagpole at school while goofing off. It was my only pair. My dad was happy sending me to school with a hole in the crotch of my pants, but thankfully my mom was able to find a patch and sew it back together.

My dad believed the Lord would provide, but he didn't believe it enough to get a job so he could help the Lord provide. So we always waited on handouts and hand-me-downs. I used to tell people he was a missionary, just not a very good one because he gave up on our family.

That left me with a sense of abandonment that lingers still. I struggle to rely on other people. Sometimes I have to work hard to not give in to the thought that I should just do everything myself, because everyone will leave anyway. Most of my siblings fared worse after he left. Being dropped like that can really stay with you.

Maybe you can see where I'm going with this. I don't mention my childhood so you'll feel sorry for me. Nor do I mention it to bash my dad; as I've told him, I've long since forgiven him. Many people out there grew up a lot harder than I did. I share this with you because I'm pretty sure this is why I relate to what shelter dogs are going through. I go into these kennels because I want these dogs to know that I understand what they're feeling. I know what it's like to be abandoned.

You can't tell from watching one of our videos, and I don't talk about it much, but I have dyslexia. I never want to use it as an excuse for anything, but I do believe that growing up with dyslexia is another aspect of my life that helped me relate to shelter dogs.

When I was pretty young, teachers put me in a special-needs class because I wasn't comprehending what I was reading. At the time, dyslexia wasn't really understood. Teachers didn't get that I could understand the subject but couldn't put the text together in my head the way other kids could. For example, the teacher would call on me in class to read a paragraph out loud. By the time I was done, the whole class was staring at me, puzzled. I had made up part of what I'd read out. I had filled in the gaps where my brain couldn't register all the words on the page. The class would hear me read a paragraph that was sort of close to what was in our readers, but not close enough for me to get away with it.

In high school, I was second seat in band. I played trumpet, and in my senior year, I made drum major. My band teacher—whom I really liked—would get upset with me because I would never push myself to make first seat. I'd settle for second or third when he thought I could have made first if I just applied myself. And he'd get frustrated because I'd ad-lib so much. He'd say, "Rocky, stop! We have a whole band here. We're all playing together. You're not the lead in a jazz band." I'd apologize and say I was just having fun. But I wasn't improvising for fun; I couldn't read music. Not even in my senior year! I wasn't content to remain second seat; I had to. I needed to let the first seat play ahead of me so I'd know what the song was, could listen to it, and then repeat the song. I'm great at playing by ear but I couldn't play you a song from a sheet of music unless you played it for me first.

In college, they had a new program for students who were dyslexic. They would allow me to write my tests in a private classroom where I could take as much time as I needed. I didn't need more time. The dyslexia didn't go away if I waited or read the questions over and over. But I did have one professor who told me he struggled with the same challenges. He taught me some tricks, like using a ruler on multiple-choice quizzes because I often filled in the wrong circle, even if I knew the answer. If I used a ruler and took it line by line, I could more accurately pick A, B, C, or D.

I was the only one in my family to go to college. I figured if everyone in my family was poor, then college was my ticket to a better life. One time in class, I was sitting next to a friend when we got a test back. I got a really bad grade. She got an A. She looked over and said, "Oh no, Rocky!" I shrugged it off like I hadn't tried. "Guess I gotta study, huh? Been out having too much fun." The thing is, I hadn't been anywhere but at home, studying. I had tried really hard to pass that test.

I barely made it through college. I took five years because I had to work full time to pay for it. And for all that, I graduated with a 2.9 grade point average. I wanted to make a great living, having grown up with so little, but when I applied to become a pharmaceutical sales rep or anything like that, I couldn't get in the door. I felt like such a loser, because the cutoff for hiring was usually a 3.0 grade point average.

I share a little bit about this because I think it also relates to the way I've come to understand dogs. So much of what dog owners learn from traditional methods of dog training doesn't apply in a high-stress shelter environment. A shelter is not a grassy yard or carefully arranged facility where well-fed and well-rested dogs are taught to heel and sit and all those very useful things. These things are worth teaching your dog, and we saw with Macy how a trainer can help in a shelter in certain circumstances. But very little of that is ever going to happen in a noisy environment, where fear and anxiety are constant obstacles to reaching a traumatized or withdrawn dog or one who's been through a hoarding situation. Chaos has taken over these animals' lives and minds, and it's far more helpful to understand where they're coming from than how they should be. It doesn't mean dog trainers or traditional training methods don't work (please, if you have learned these methods or are a dog trainer volunteer at a shelter, we need you!), but with that said, all my life I've been told how I "should be," and sorry, but I just don't fit in that bucket.

And neither do the shelter dogs who need the most help.

If you don't fit in that bucket–maybe because you've got a condition like mine, or you're not "book smart," or maybe you're off-the-charts smart and don't feel like you belong–whatever it is, you can use that to help. You don't need to be a dog trainer. Take your genuine self to a shelter and you might be surprised by what you can do! Even if you don't feel comfortable getting into a kennel because you're scared of big dogs, or all dogs, there's still so much you can do to make it a little easier for shelter staff to do their jobs. If you've ever felt like you want to help, then you are the perfect person to help.

Are you good at accounting? Shelters need help keeping their books in order. Are you a handyman? Shelters always have things that need fixing. Are you a good salesperson? You could help raise donations. Whatever you're good at, whatever your strengths, a shelter can use what you have to offer.

One of the reasons we're compelled to help, I think, is that dogs are such a reflection of who we are. I talked previously in the book about how sitting with dogs has helped me get over the trauma of my stroke, especially the nightmares. The difficult experiences we've been through can help us help others. Maybe you're going through something now, and it's leaving you asking some tough questions, like what the meaning of life is. Getting outside of yourself and helping others, you might be amazed at how much it helps you–how much meaning it brings us.

You don't need to quit your job and go all-in. Start small. Volunteer in the evenings or on weekends. You'll see how even just a little time makes a tremendous impact for the dogs and for you.

---

Not every shelter is going to let you walk in and sit in their kennels. I started by seeing the problems and the challenges in the shelter system and trying to help in little but effective ways. When I started The Dog Bakery, I was bringing dogs from shelters into our stores to help them get adopted. Every time one found a home, my staff and I celebrated.

I'd go back to the shelter to take on another dog, and there'd be more replacing the one we'd already helped. I began to recognize how big the problem was. This was decades ago, and shelters have only become more crowded since. I knew I needed to reach more people in order to keep up with the need. It took time to figure that out and build up our following online.

What drove me, though, and what can fuel you too, was the fulfillment and joy I found in this work from the day I started, even when just volunteering in little ways. Sure, sometimes I was rejected. Know that if you start offering your time to shelters, some of them will say thanks but no thanks. Shelters aren't well-run businesses focused on customer service. They're not community outreach programs. Shelters are loosely held-together organizations that try their best to help with an impossible situation: too many dogs, not enough homes.

Just a few months before writing this, I was rejected by a shelter I was offering to help. It didn't matter that I could bring them donations, awareness, and support–sometimes they just don't have time to accept what you're willing to give. And that's okay. I still love them for what they do, and this might happen to you, but if it does just move on and try another one. Or, if you were rejected in the past, go back and revisit them. Shelters' and rescues' situations can change daily.

Shelters need you to do this. *I* need you to do this or your own version of what I'm doing to help. And no, I don't get territorial about it. People ask me if it's okay that they do what

I do. They don't want to step on my toes or steal my thing. It's not my thing! It's everyone's thing. We can be so much stronger for these animals if we all do whatever we can together.

So be resilient, and don't be offended if you can't walk in and do what you imagined. Even if they ask you to clean the glass doors of the kennels, go ahead. Again, start small. You're making a difference. You're keeping the place clean so that when potential adopters come in, they can imagine the dog in their home and not get caught up thinking about how dirty the dog could make it.

Small things help in big ways.

Maybe you do want a dog. *And* you want to help a whole bunch of dogs. Here's a simple solution: fostering.

Fostering got me involved early on, and it helped me learn what it was like to be with different kinds of dogs, because different breeds have different personalities and bring different dynamics to a household. It also helps you understand what it's like to care for dogs with special needs. Even with two dogs already and a baby on the way, who could have guessed we'd love a blind Cane Corso so much we'd adopt one who had a bad heart! Fostering can not only teach you about different dogs, but what you're capable of yourself. The troubles you've come through might be a superpower in disguise.

Maybe you're afraid you'd fail at fostering because you would never be able to give a dog up after a few months. But the thing is, they need you, and you will need to make a promise to yourself when you foster a dog that you will help that dog get to their forever family. Remember how we fell in love with Moose, just sitting in a kennel with him? Can you imagine how hard it would be to say goodbye if we'd brought him to the farm for a few months? You can't keep them, because you have to open your home for the next dog.

Now, there is one instance where you *can* keep a foster dog. Maybe you're fostering because you're trying to figure out what kind of dog would be right for you to adopt. Here's a pro tip: Fostering can give you a chance to try out a dog that you think might fit with your lifestyle. You will learn things about different kinds of dogs that you love and other things you could live without. If you want a couch potato of a dog, you're going to learn that certain dogs, like an English Bulldog, fit that lifestyle, and certain dogs, like a Blue Heeler, never sit still. "What a cute little dog," you might think–until you find yourself looking for ways to keep that dog active 12 hours a day! You might learn that you love big dogs when you thought you could only handle a small dog. Fostering is a great way to find out without making a long-term commitment you're worried you can't keep.

Reach out to your local rescue or shelter and ask how you apply to foster. Don't worry about whether you have the perfect home situation. Don't worry about anyone judging you or about not knowing enough about dogs. Maybe you've never even had a dog. That's okay. Are you willing to learn? Rescues and shelters need all kinds of situations. You live in a small apartment? No problem. A little Yorkie could be perfect for a

***Flip being a good boy.***

first-time foster (of course, check with your landlord to be sure you can have dogs). Just put yourself out there. And remember, it's okay to get rejected. Some shelters or rescues are more strict than they need to be. And some aren't strict enough! There's a place for you if you're willing to go find it.

Yes, when a foster dog leaves it's hard. When you really like the dog, it can feel like someone ripped off your arm. I couldn't have been happier to see Bean adopted by the very person who'd found him in the first place, but after our journey with him and the effort to fix his badly broken leg, I really struggled with letting him go. Then there was Princess, the German Shepherd. Watching her meet her forever family was one of the most rewarding days of my life. And knowing Valerie learned what it was like to be truly cared for while she was in this world turned a sad ending into a small miracle of kindness and love.

You will get more out of fostering dogs than they will ever get out of you. Making the space in your life for a foster dog—or an adopted dog—opens up all the best things in a person. I've gotten comments from people online asking why I'm not helping homeless people instead of dogs, as if I love dogs more than I love people. I reject that line of thinking—I like dogs and people and helping both. In my experience, the more you love and the more you give, the more capacity you grow to love and to give. It's not an either/or decision.

Helping people, helping pets. Loving dogs, loving people. If you open your heart, you will be rewarded and surprised and fulfilled. It will change your life, as it has mine, and you will be amazed at how much love and capacity for love you have. I wish everyone could have the opportunity to foster at least one dog in their lifetime. I can't recommend it enough.

Thank you for being with me, with all of us, on this journey—the book, social media, wherever we meet.

Kelly says hi! Kobe is settling on his blanket. The kids are in bed. It's time to get some rest, because tomorrow we've got dogs to meet, check on, and play with. And we want to be ready to enjoy every minute we spend with them, because—and believe me, this is true—life is just better with dogs.

Now go find out for yourself!

# ACKNOWLEDGMENTS

I have been lucky in my life to have people who have given of themselves to help me find my footing along the way. Without them I do not believe my path would have led to where I am, and for that I would like to express my deepest *Mahalo Nui Loa* (thank you so very much) to the following people who made this book possible:

**First and foremost, my amazing wife, Kelly:** Thank you for being the kind of person whose laugh fills a room, whose spirit lights up the darkest day, and whose beauty–inside and out–still stops me in my tracks. You're the full package, and somehow I got lucky enough to walk through life with you. You've seen me at my lowest and lifted me up without hesitation. When I'm chasing the clouds, you're right there beside me matching my energy beat for beat. You've never laughed at my crazy ideas–you've leaned in, encouraged them, and believed in me. When we met, I didn't have much to offer except maybe a few wild dreams and a love for animals. But you saw something in me. And every single day I work hard to prove you right. Thank you for being my partner, my rock, my safe place. And thank you for everything you do for our family. I couldn't do this–any of this–without you.

**My beautiful children:** When you came into the world, my heart expanded and grew in ways I didn't know were possible. Thank you for giving me a true sense of fulfillment. Seeing the world through your eyes and sharing this part of my life with you makes the mission so much more rewarding. Your laughs, love, and amazement at the little things bring me tremendous joy. I'm so proud to be your dad.

**Mom:** Thank you for selflessly giving so much of your life and for always being there for me, no matter what. You taught me tenacity, unconditional love, and how to navigate through hardship. And to my stepdad, Dave, thank you for being so giving, understanding, and supportive of Mom and all of us kids.

**My loyal friends:** Q, Topher, and Kahipaokalani. From bagging groceries, to building barns and riding bikes, thank you for the happy memories and lifetime of friendship.

**My team:** Thank you to Chad for helping bring this book to life and believing wholeheartedly in this mission, and thank you to my entire team. I am constantly in awe of your talent, hard work, and passion.

**A special animal shelter:** To the shelter I am constantly drawn back to because of an amazing group of people giving so much to save animals daily. Chief Mo and her entire team at Animal Friends of the Valleys–thank you!

**My namesake:** A special thank you to Auntie Nona Beamer. I am truly blessed to have received your blessing of my name, which has given me purpose and has been a part of saving many animals' lives.

**And you, the reader:** Thank you for your kindness, your open heart, and your willingness to see the magic in these deserving souls. Whether you're celebrating your own rescue dog or considering welcoming one into your life, you are part of the ripple effect of good in this world. There's only one thing in this world that will provide you with unconditional love, and it wags its tail.

**Thank you all from the bottom of my heart.**

# INDEX

## A



## B

## C



## D



## E



## F

## G

## H

## I

## K

## L



## M

## N



## O



## P



## R



## S

## W–Z

# LEARN MORE ABOUT ROCKY AND THE PRODUCTS THAT SUPPORT HIS MISSION!

## ROCKY'S PRODUCTS

Rocky's all-natural jerky and chews are made in the USA with human-grade ingredients. Every purchase helps support Flip Farms, which provides rehabilitation for shelter dogs.

www.shoprockykanaka.com

SCAN HERE TO LEARN MORE

## FLIP FARMS

Flip Farms is a safe haven where shelter dogs can heal, train, and prepare for their forever homes. Through care, love and rehabilitation, we give underserved dogs a fresh start.

www.rockykanaka.com/flipfarms

SCAN HERE TO LEARN MORE

## FLIP COFFEE

Every cup supports shelter dog rehabilitation at Flip Farms, giving them the care they need to find loving homes. The smooth, low-acid coffee is small-batch roasted and USDA Organic.

www.flipcoffee.com

SCAN HERE TO LEARN MORE

## THE DOG BAKERY

In addition to rescuing shelter dogs, Rocky is a pet chef and owner of The Dog Bakery in Southern California, where he crafts fresh-baked, all-natural treats for pups.

www.thedogbakery.com

SCAN HERE TO LEARN MORE

FIND YOUR SOUL DOG!
Every year, countless dogs are euthanized—not because they're unlovable, but because they've never found a home. But many can still be saved.
Whether you're a shelter looking to list adoptable dogs or a future pet parent searching for the perfect match, scan the code to connect with dogs in need—free of charge—through RockyKanaka.com.
YOUR PERFECT PET IS OUT THERE! START YOUR ADOPTION JOURNEY TODAY!

**ROCKY KANAKA** is the host and creator of the popular YouTube series Sitting with Dogs, which he uses to shine a much-needed light on shelter dogs waiting for adoption, and to support pet rescues and volunteering. With his fanbase of more than 10 million subscribers and followers online, the Emmy-nominated TV host, pet chef, and entrepreneur can often be found serving cakes and treats to dogs at his Los Angeles store, The Dog Bakery. Along with his wife, Kelly, he recently launched Flip Coffee, a coffee brand named after his late, beloved Boxer. Grown at their property in north San Diego County, the coffee is sold in support of Flip Farms, a newly built dog rehabilitation center—also named in tribute to Flip, a mentor and guide to the many dogs fostered in the Kanaka household. Raised between the islands of Hawaii and the plains of Missouri, Rocky moved to Los Angeles in 2003. He and Kelly are pet parents to Kobe, a blind Cane Corso, and all the foster dogs they rehabilitate on Flip Farms until they find their forever homes.